Vertical Differentia　　　　　Gifted, Advanced, and High-Potential Students

Vertical Differentiation for Gifted, Advanced, and High-Potential Students outlines 25 engaging tools and strategies to stretch student thinking, promote deep learning, and provide layers of challenge in the classroom and beyond.

Each strategy is expertly designed to foster deep inquiry and conceptual understanding by guiding students to justify conclusions, apply critical and creative thinking, develop solutions to real-world problems, and transfer learning across contexts. Packed with both "tried and true" thinking models and new, innovative ideas with concrete examples, this resource ensures that no matter where students are in their learning journey, they'll find themselves challenged and engaged.

This book is essential reading for educators looking to support and extend student thinking across content areas and grade levels.

Emily L. Mofield is Assistant Professor in the College of Education at Lipscomb University, USA. She has over 20 years of experience in the field of gifted education in a variety of roles including teacher, district leader, researcher, assistant professor, and author.

Vertical Differentiation for Gifted, Advanced, and High-Potential Students

25 Strategies to Stretch Student Thinking

Emily L. Mofield

Routledge
Taylor & Francis Group

NEW YORK AND LONDON

Cover image: @ Getty Images

First published 2023
by Routledge
605 Third Avenue, New York, NY 10158

and by Routledge
4 Park Square, Milton Park, Abingdon, Oxon, OX14 4RN

Routledge is an imprint of the Taylor & Francis Group, an informa business

Library of Congress Cataloging-in-Publication Data
A catalog record for this book has been requested

ISBN: 978-1-032-27559-8 (hbk)
ISBN: 978-1-032-27558-1 (pbk)
ISBN: 978-1-003-29328-6 (ebk)

DOI: 10.4324/9781003293286

Typeset in Palatino
by Apex CoVantage, LLC

Access the Support Material: www.routledge.com/9781032275581

This is dedicated to all the committed teachers who strive to spot talent in young people, nurture their strengths, and unleash potential! Find the light and fan the flame!

Soli deo gloria

Contents

Acknowledgements

I would like to acknowledge the many teachers who have implemented these strategies with students! Thank you for your feedback and suggestions for fine-tuning these strategies to be most readily applicable. I acknowledge that many of these strategies in this book are "tried and true" to the field, and so, I am thankful for the established work of the original authors these models (e.g., Richard Paul, Linda Elder, Edward de Bono, Bob Eberle, Hilda Taba, etc.). I hope to present them in a way that shows how they apply to planning instruction supporting the progression from novice learning to expertise by building powerful mental models. I also hope these strategies are applied to provide opportunities for high-potential students to access rigorous instruction.

I must acknowledge my scholarly heroes whose work has helped me understand gifted education in the context of talent development: Joyce Van-Tassel-Baska, Tamra Stambaugh, Paula Olszewski-Kubilius, and Todd Kettler. Their work has certainly influenced my thinking in regard to purposes of gifted curriculum as a means to identify, support, and grow talent.

Acknowledgements

List of Resources

About the Author

Emily Mofield, EdD, is an assistant professor at Lipscomb University, Nashville, Tennessee, where she co-leads the graduate program in Gifted and Advanced Academics. Emily has over 20 years of experience in gifted education as a gifted education teacher, leader, researcher, and assistant professor. She has served as the Curriculum Studies network chair for NAGC and has co-authored numerous NAGC award-winning advanced language arts curriculum units (with Tamra Stambaugh, Vanderbilt Programs for Talented Youth). She is also the author/co-author of several research publications and book chapters related to achievement motivation, collaborative teaching practices, and curriculum design. She is the co-recipient of the NAGC Hollingworth Award for Excellence in Research and the Texas Association for Gifted and Talented 2019 Legacy Book Award for *Teaching Tenacity, Resilience, and a Drive for Excellence* (with Megan Parker Peters). She has also co-authored *Collaboration, Coaching, and Coteaching in Gifted Education* (2021 NAGC Book of the Year – Practitioner Category, with Vicki Phelps). She has most recently published *A Teacher's Guide to Curriculum Design for Gifted and Advanced Learners* (with Tamra Stambaugh) and working on a 2023 release of *Coaching in Gifted Education: Tools for Building Capacity and Catalyzing Change* (with Vicki Phelps).

Emily regularly provides consultation and leads professional learning addressing collaborative teaching and use of differentiation strategies for advanced learners for school districts, conferences, and special groups. She also serves on the advisory board for the Javits Grant: Project BUMP UP on collaborative practices in gifted education. Emily is also the recipient of the Jo Patterson Service Award and Curriculum Award from the Tennessee Association for the Gifted, and the 2021 Dean's Award from the College of Education of Lipscomb University for significant contributions to the field of education.

Introduction

They say to write the book you wish you had. This is indeed my aim. From my experiences in teaching teachers in a variety of contexts, I have wanted to share a resource that describes the many strategies and tools that provide additional layers of challenge to the standard curriculum and promote deep engagement of learning. Many of these strategies are "tried and true" to many in gifted education, and others are designed to promote deep learning and the transfer of knowledge to new contexts and real-world situations. This deep learning and transfer occur when students have opportunities to think critically, make connections, and reflect on their own thinking. In doing so, they develop the habits of an expert as they analyze and evaluate the interrelationships of concepts and how these concepts apply to new contexts.

All students need opportunities to use higher-order thinking and engage in deep learning, though it is important to remember that students enter the classroom with a wide range of readiness levels. Gifted students often need less practice on a skill to reach mastery, and so they are ready to dive deeper into content, go beyond surface level learning, and examine complex issues related to the content. When embedded with advanced content, the strategies in this book are designed to stretch students so that they continue to grow and progress in their learning. No matter where students are in their learning trajectory, there's always a next step, and these strategies provide the next level of stretch and support.

This book might be helpful for gifted education teachers designing curriculum units, regular education teachers who teach cluster groups of gifted

DOI: 10.4324/9781003293286-1

students (e.g., five to six gifted students within a classroom), or advanced/honors teachers who seek ways to differentiate the scope and sequence from standard vs. honors courses. Many of these strategies can also be used to differentiate instruction within a multi-systems support model (such as response-to-intervention (RTI)) to challenge advanced learners. Additionally, this book can serve any teacher seeking to increase the level of cognitive rigor in classroom instruction. Instructional design starts with understanding the learner, so we must ask, where is the learner in relation to the learning goal? For many gifted and high-potential students, they may have already arrived at this destination, or they need more "friction" along the way to grapple with the content at more complex levels, preparing them to think as experts within a discipline. This is what is meant by "vertical differentiation" (see Chapter 1).

Much is said about the importance of critical and creative thinking in education. These words are often tossed around PLCs, boasted as educational system goals, and emphasized as important to 21st-century learning skills. Yet, when it comes down to teaching students how to think this way and apply it to content, there is often a disconnect between the aim and the action. VanTassel-Baska et al. (2020) conducted a study to evaluate the prevalence and effectiveness of differentiation practices in 329 classrooms in six school districts. These school districts selected had well-established gifted programs and a prevalence of advanced programs. Their findings showed that differentiation through the use of high-level thinking (critical thinking, creative thinking, and analytical thinking) were observed in relatively low instances. The study noted that in most cases, differentiation was not applied in whole class or small group work for advanced learners in elementary and middle school cluster-grouped classrooms. Differentiated teaching behaviors such as using models for thinking, using strategies for synthesis of information, applying diverse points of view, using imagination, building arguments in multiple forms, and drawing inferences were "not observed" for 60% or more of the time in the classrooms. They also noted that advanced learners' needs were more likely to be addressed when teachers used differentiated curricula.

Given these findings, it is likely that teachers need support in knowing the strategies and models to use with advanced learners. How exactly can lessons be planned to build arguments in multiple forms and to teach strategies for applying diverse points of view? What if teachers had examples of applying these strategies to various content areas? This book is designed to show examples of what it looks like to teach analytical, critical, and creative thinking explicitly with content so that the elusive ideas of differentiated instruction can become more concrete. Such differentiated instruction can be applied to accommodate for individual differences or as a way to design differentiated curriculum for groups of advanced learners (e.g., in cluster settings, part of multi-system support models, or advanced/honors courses). Additionally, these strategies can be used by any teacher seeking to prepare students for rigorous content. These strategies can be used to build strong mental models (i.e., schema), support the development and use of academic language, and make abstract concepts "concrete."

The National Association for Gifted Children (NAGC) Programming Standards (NAGC, 2019) highlights the need for educators to differentiate, accelerate, and/or expand content standards. The strategies in this book align well with these standards. For example, the evidence-based practice for Standard 3.4.3. indicates, "Educators use models of inquiry to engage students in critical thinking, creative thinking, and problem-solving strategies, particularly in their domain(s) of talent, both to reveal and address the needs of students with gifts and talents." The forthcoming chapters provide numerous examples for planning differentiated curriculum and instruction with various models.

Organization of the Book

This book begins with an overview of vertical differentiation. In Chapter 1, the Vertical Differentiation Model outlines a path for students to dive deeper into content by moving from simple facts to more complex ideas, from concrete to more abstract conceptual understanding, and from basic application to more strategic reasoning in order to transfer their learning to real-world contexts. This is demonstrated in light of Webb's Depth of Knowledge framework which is described as a structure for thinking about increasing the cognitive expectations for students to engage in a task.

Chapter 2 provides an explanation of learning goals (know, understand, and do) as a base for designing differentiated tasks followed by an overview of critical and creative thinking models. These models are embedded within the structure of many of the strategies presented in the forthcoming chapters. Then, Stretch Prompts are introduced as a way to "stretch" students to engage more deeply with content with built-in tiers for extended learning, transfer, and reasoning.

Chapter 3 focuses on analysis strategies as approaches to build a student's schema in making connections among concepts and understanding the underlying structure of content. Additionally, strategies for close analysis of texts and other content are provided to ignite inquiry and provide opportunities for students to generalize big ideas to other contexts.

Chapter 4 provides structures for problem identification, guiding students to understand the underlying cause-effect relationships and evaluate short- and long-term consequences of a problem or solution. These strategies can be used to guide students to dive deeper into the "why" behind various problems providing a foundation for solving a problem. Chapter 5 then provides a number of strategies for developing creative solutions and evaluating them on established criteria.

Chapter 6 includes a number of ideas for making creative, insightful connections by linking new ideas to known ideas. These strategies are presented within the context of metaphors as mental models used to strengthen and support expert-like thinking.

Chapter 7 provides structures for supporting students in developing and evaluating logical arguments. Multiple models are presented as ways for students to build arguments to support a claim and "justify and explain why" their reasoning is valid.

Chapter 8 focuses on supporting metacognition with strategies that emphasize students' reflections of *how* they learn. When individuals are aware of their own thinking processes, they can regulate their thoughts and actions to maximize learning and performance. This chapter also includes a number of strategies to promote awareness of regulating emotion in the process of learning. Becoming aware of emotion allows us to manage emotion and move forward with resilience.

Chapter 9 provides guidance on developing differentiated tasks by incorporating the strategies from the previous chapters. Ideas for assessments and vertically differentiated choice-based tasks are provided. The chapter concludes with considerations of scaffolds for students from diverse backgrounds and students who are twice-exceptional to build access to advanced learning opportunities.

The appendix provides a list of references that show support for the use of the strategies and models. These resources show evidence of the effectiveness of the model/strategy or theoretical rationale for its use. The research around high-quality curriculum for gifted students (VanTassel-Baska, 2018, pp. 73–75) shows effective results for student learning when the following features are in place: 1) scaffolds that support higher-level thinking, 2) sustained lessons that use higher-level thinking, 3) questions that emphasize analysis, synthesis, and evaluation, 4) assessments that are advanced, open-ended, and require Problem Solving, 5) the use of integration of skills and higher-level concepts within content, 6) the use of metacognition for reflection, and 7) the use of multicultural readings and materials. The aim of this book is to provide concrete ideas for using these features, particularly in supporting questioning, high-level thinking, and the use of models so that students learn to be innovative thinkers who change the world.

Though many of these strategies in this text are not new to gifted education, I aim to present them through the lens of the talent development model (Subotnik et al., 2011). The strategies are presented to guide students to perceive structures, extend patterns, make connections, plan strategically, and reflect on their own thinking processes. In doing so, students are prepared to transfer content learning to new contexts. This is what experts do, and this is what we can teach students to do as we vertically differentiate "up" in planning and instruction.

1

What is Vertical Differentiation?

Recently, the "Future of Jobs" report noted that the top skills for future work include complex problem solving, critical thinking and analysis, and creativity (World Economic Forum, 2020). Self-management, reasoning, and leadership/social influence also make the list. As educators, we must ask ourselves, to what extent are we preparing students to obtain these skills? Do students have opportunities to engage in deep learning so that they eventually use their knowledge to produce new ideas? How are we equipping students to solve complex problems of tomorrow when adults do not even know how to grapple with the complexities of today? We must immerse students in meaningful learning and engagement now so they can step into this future with adaptability and strength. The strategies described in this book can be used to stimulate and challenge students in their thinking by fostering inquiry and deep conceptual understanding. This includes guiding students to justify conclusions, apply critical and creative thinking, develop solutions to real-world problems, and transfer learning to multiple conditions and contexts.

Do all students benefit from these methods of teaching? Absolutely! There really is no such thing as a strategy that *only* works with gifted learners. To be clear, these strategies can open doors and opportunities for a broader population of students, not just those who are formally identified as "gifted." When students are exposed to rich learning experiences that foster deep learning in a content area, it is an opportunity to observe how specific student strengths emerge. In this way, students demonstrate a potential, or *possibility*, of future talent (and so, they are often called "high-potential" students). A student's true potential is unknown until opportunities are provided and taken. Thus,

DOI: 10.4324/9781003293286-2

these strategies serve to be an *opportunity* for the very capacity of a student's potential to expand.

These strategies indeed apply to teaching gifted and advanced students (as noted in the title). When developing curriculum and planning instruction for students who already know and understand the basic skills and facts, their next steps in learning should be to engage in the content in a way that stretches their thinking. Often, gifted learners enter the classroom with advanced readiness compared to their peers. To continue to progress in their learning, they benefit from accelerated content, higher order processing, and opportunities to connect the content to abstract concepts or big ideas around the discipline (VanTassel-Baska & Baska, 2019). In essence, they need instruction that is different: differentiated instruction.

Traditionally in gifted education, differentiation is often justified as a response to gifted learners' behaviors or characteristics. Because gifted students learn at a fast pace and comprehend complex ideas, they need opportunities to explore content in-depth, manipulate ideas, and make connections across concepts. Models of differentiation for gifted learners typically involve modifying the content, process, and product (Maker, 1982; Tomlinson et al., 2002). Modifying the content means accelerating the content, teaching more advanced concepts, and integrating content to concepts and themes, providing opportunities for students to generalize ideas within and across disciplines. Modifying the process involves structuring questioning and thinking to include an active exploration of ideas, open inquiry, and thinking about content in more complex and abstract ways (e.g., high levels of Bloom's taxonomy—evaluate, analyze, create). Modifying the product means providing students opportunities to demonstrate what they learned in a variety of ways, especially as it relates to synthesizing information, addressing real-world problems, and developing authentic products in ways that mirror what experts think and do. Modifying the content, process, and product has been the go-to approach for differentiation in gifted education for some time. It is traditionally viewed as a way to alleviate a "need," but as I share in the remaining portions of this book, differentiation can serve broader purposes in the context of cultivating students' strengths and talents.

Differentiation in Light of Talent Development

In the talent development framework of gifted education (Subotnik et al., 2011), differentiation is not simply a response to addressing a student's need, but a *means* to develop talent and nurture strengths by providing advanced curricular experiences. The nuance is an important one. As Kettler (2016) explained, when we discuss programming for highly skilled football players, artists, or performers, we are not so concerned with "need-meeting." Instead, coaches and directors of fine arts programs are concerned with developing elite talent by providing experiences that grow and strengthen players' and artists' skills to more sophisticated levels. Likewise, with advanced students, developing their talents involves providing rich learning experiences that allow them to sharpen their skills in specific content domains. Modifying the content, process, and products not only "meets their needs" but nurtures their skills and talents to more advanced levels of performance. In this way, "needs" are addressed as a *means* to developing talent (Kettler, 2016).

Unfortunately, differentiation in the classroom is not always practically translated into modified content, process, and products to a degree that is both interesting and challenging for gifted students. If you google "differentiation for gifted" you will find a number of well-intended practical ideas such as developing choice-boards and menus showcasing a variety of product options for students. However, a careful examination of these tasks too often reveals "diluted differentiation" because the tasks lack sufficient depth and complexity that stretch and extend students' thinking. We must consider if the tasks are complex enough to prepare students to think, write, and construct knowledge in ways that experts do.

Throughout this book, I emphasize that "vertical differentiation" serves to nurture strengths and talents through exposure to high-level content and through experiences where the learner is introduced to creating, practicing, and thinking as an expert within a discipline.

Vertical Differentiation

Challenge, Not Just Choice

I use the term "vertical differentiation" to mean *adjusting "up" what students know, understand, and do by providing challenges where students are grappling with cognitively complex tasks that prepare them to create, practice, and think as an expert.* Vertical differentiation is not simply about providing choices regarding the content or product, rather, it is about providing the challenge.

Fortunately, we can provide both choice and challenge in student learning when we thoughtfully include opportunities to solve problems, make decisions, and develop new understanding using tools of the discipline. The aim for vertical differentiation is to provide contexts for students to be cognitively engaged. Cognitive engagement refers to the "psychological effort students put into learning and mastering content" (Fisher et al., 2018, p. 135). When we intentionally plan complex tasks that elicit deep understanding and abstract thinking, students engage in the heavy lifting of learning and grow.

Create tasks that force students to THINK!

I like to think about differentiation in terms of quadrants. As noted in Figure 1.1, Quadrant III is illustrative of "boring and bland" curriculum. This might include a typical assignment that all students do, that is neither appealing to their interests, nor is it at a level of sufficient challenge to push students to grow. In Quadrant IV, tasks and assignments are differentiated by choice, but not necessarily differentiated with more challenge. In this context, I would call this "horizontal" differentiation. Students are provided choices of activities that are interesting (e.g., build a model, create art, sing a song), but students do not have opportunities to engage in deep learning of the content. These types of activities are often found in choice menus or tic-tac-toe menus, but it is important to examine if such activities fall in Quadrant IV, "fluff and stuff."

In Quadrant II, tasks and assignments are "bumped up" a notch to provide a more rigorous learning experience at a level of student readiness, but they are not necessarily tied to students' interests or lead to authentic learning experiences. In this quadrant, we may see students "going through the motions" of school. The work is challenging but not necessarily intellectually stimulating. Students may be assigned tasks that require them to analyze, evaluate, and synthesize, all skills for higher-order processing, but they are limited to one way of showing what they know through tasks such as a five-paragraph essay or a prescriptive presentation. Here, we often see "compliant learning." Students comply and do what they are asked to do, though their motivation to persevere may wane. Though better than the basic

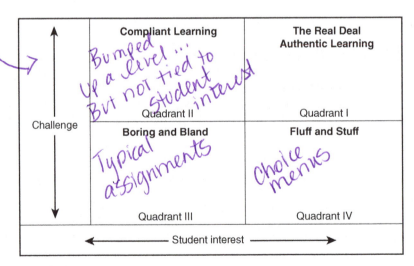

Figure 1.1 Vertical Differentiation Quadrants

Source: Republished with permission of Taylor and Francis, from Collaboration, Coteaching, and Coaching in Gifted Education: Sharing Strategies to Support Gifted Learners, Mofield, E., & Phelps, V. (2020), permission conveyed through Copyright Clearance Center, Inc.

"boring and bland" Cornflakes, this type of Shredded Wheat learning lacks opportunities for students to deeply engage with the content in ways that incite curiosity, develop a sense of agency, and inspire future learning.

In Quadrant I, students have opportunities to explore the content related to their interests or strengths while also applying conceptual understanding of the content to real-world contexts through problem solving, critical thinking, and creative applications. This is a protein-packed breakfast (bacon and eggs!) with fruit on the side selected by the student from a breakfast buffet. This is the "good stuff" where students are challenged and intellectually stimulated as they engage in content in meaningful ways. Here, they are invested in their own learning as they have opportunities to make decisions, problem solve, ask new questions, and reflect on their learning and growth.

Vertical Differentiation Aligned to Visible Learning

So, how do we plan for Quadrant I, the real deal? This is what the chapters that follow are all about. Through bumping up what we ask students to know, understand, and do, and providing options for students to "show what you know," we can guide students toward learning that is transferable, applies to real-world contexts, and introduces students to skills to "think as an expert."

Figure 1.2 presents a visual for moving towards this real-world transfer through the advanced content, conceptual understanding, and high-level thinking. This model combines features of the Integrated Curriculum Model (advanced content, process, and concept; VanTassel-Baska & Baska, 2019) with Hattie et al.'s (2017) visible learning approaches (surface, deep, and transfer learning).

Within the visible learning framework, Hattie et al. (2017) explain differences between surface, deep, and transfer learning. Surface learning is described as the introduction of new skills and concepts that lead to initial conceptual understanding. This is an important step in the learning process and should not be confused with superficial learning (e.g., low-level learning or memorization). Students need to understand examples, non-examples, labels, and misconceptions of new content. The next stage, deep learning, occurs when students consolidate their surface learning and make connections among concepts. At this stage, students elaborate on their conceptual understandings, make generalizations, and think flexibly about concepts. Then, transfer learning occurs when students apply their learning and thinking to real-world contexts. Hattie's (2017) visible learning meta-analyses also show that transfer strategies are one of the strongest factors associated with

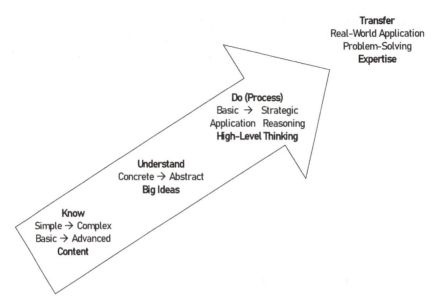

Figure 1.2 Vertical Differentiation Model

student achievement (showing a large effect size of .86). The Vertical Differentiation Model shows a path for dialing up instruction as students move from simple facts to more complex ideas, from concrete to more abstract conceptual understanding, and from basic application to more strategic reasoning that allows for the transfer of learning to real-world contexts.

First Steps

When planning instruction for any learner, we must know where they are in relation to the learning goal. Differentiation simply cannot happen without pre-assessment. Teachers can pre-assess in several ways: using an end-of-unit assessment, asking students to complete the "Five Most Difficult" problems (see Winebrenner, 2001), asking students to develop a concept map to show their understanding of the relationship between ideas, or developing a short pre-assessment around the unit goals of what students should know, do, and understand.

If students demonstrate that they already know the material, then teachers can "compact" the curriculum by providing opportunities for students to move ahead in the curriculum sequence (accelerate the content), allowing the students to work on a high-interest activity such as an independent investigation or providing enrichment or a tiered assignment so students can dive deeper into the related content. The chapters that follow provide ideas and strategies that can be used to create tiered tasks and assignments for students who have exceptional strengths in content areas and who might benefit from opportunities to go more in-depth with content.

ABC's for Vertical Differentiation

After learning where your students are in relation to learning goals and mastery of standards, you can use the ABCs of differentiation to begin planning for "vertical" differentiation. As shown in Table 1.1, the ABCs include Advance the Content, Build the Buy-In, and Create the Challenge.

A—Advance the Content is essential for differentiating for gifted learners. As previously stated, the strategies in this book are not necessarily "gifted" strategies that work only with gifted students, however, when higher-level thinking processes are paired with content that is above-grade level, the cognitive demands will likely be a suitable match to challenge the student within their zone of proximal development. As noted in Table 1.1, this can include accelerating the pace, using advanced resources, and exposing students to materials and texts experts within the field might use.

B—Build the Buy-In is about differentiating based on what students want to learn and why. Teachers can provide advanced texts and complex critical thinking tasks all the live-long day, but this bumped up challenge does not necessarily ignite motivation for a student to engage with the content. As discussed with the cereal metaphor, tasks and assignments for gifted students might be labeled as "rigorous" (remember the Shredded Wheat?) as we know they are "good" for the gifted learner, but unless student interests, strengths, funds of knowledge, and motivations are considered through providing choices for students, it is less likely a student will sustain effort over time to complete the challenging tasks.

Building the buy-in happens when we know and understand what students value. Wigfield and Eccles's (1992) work on achievement motivation points to various types of task value:

◆ Attainment value is based on a student's identity. We often see this when a student might be highly motivated to achieve as an athlete because the student sees herself as an athlete. Maintaining the identity of doing what athletes do is extremely valuable to the student.

Table 1.1 ABCs of Differentiation

Advance the Content	Build Buy-In	Creating Challenge

• Accelerate the content and pace
• Provide advanced resources
• Introduce advanced vocabulary/concepts
• Content-specific expert-like thinking
	• Build in choices
	• Harness motivation
	• Create task value:
	  – Tied to identity
	  – Tied to interest
	  – Tied to future
	  – Worth time and effort
	  – Tied to real-world
		• Open inquiry
		• Depth/Complexity
		• Critical thinking
		• Creative thinking
		• High-level thinking
		• Conceptual thinking
		• Posing boundaries
		• Transfer

- Intrinsic value is based on interests. Intrinsic value refers to having a strong inclination to various topics because the student finds such topics inherently interesting.
- Utility value is based on how meaningful the learning will be in the future. For example, a student might be motivated to do well in AP History because he knows the course will prepare him for success in college.
- Cost is based on considering if the task is worth the time and effort.

As you plan for student learning, you can appeal to any and all of these types of task value as you link content to students' lives and their future. Through providing choices or opportunities for students to provide their input into their learning, students can "buy-in" to its value as they become learners who see themselves with agency and potential.

C—Create the Challenge involves planning for students to think, reason, problem solve, and construct meaning from the content. Each of these ways to "create challenge" is illustrated through the strategies within this book. These features are often cited through gifted education literature as important "processing skills" for planning instruction for gifted learners. One or many of these features can be incorporated within learning experiences and student tasks. These can also serve as a planning guide for developing a unit, lesson, assignment, or student product. Table 1.2 provides definitions and example applications for "create a challenge" in vertical differentiation.

Table 1.2 Features of "Creating Challenge"

	Meaning	Example Application
Open inquiry	Develop tasks with few parameters where students explore issues or problems.	Implement problem-based learning around the issue of the honeybee population decreasing. Students examine and define the problem and develop multiple solutions.
Depth	Extend learning through examining trends, issues, and patterns within a discipline (Kaplan, 2009). Justify or construct a reasoned argument to develop a conclusion (VanTassel-Baska & Stambaugh, 2006).	Pose a problem or issue (e.g., Should farmers continue to use pesticides to increase food yield?). Students construct and justify arguments with multiple sources.
Complexity	Make connections among multiple ideas; observe inter-relationships between concepts; and understand multiple perspectives (Kaplan, 2009; VanTassel-Baska & Stambaugh, 2006).	Ask students to examine how the decreased bee population is the result of multiple factors and how it affects social, economic, and cultural systems.
Critical thinking	Use reason and logic to analyze, evaluate, and construct arguments.	Critically analyze the pros, cons, biased perspectives, and effects of using pesticides and/or genetically modified crops.
Creative thinking	Look at problems with new perspectives with an aim to create something new.	Develop multiple creative solutions for increasing the honeybee population and elaborating in detail how an original solution addresses the issue.
High-level thinking	Analyze, evaluate, or synthesize information (from Bloom's taxonomy)	Students analyze multiple causes and effects of the bee population decreasing, evaluating effects on various points of view (farmers, environmentalists, consumers), and create an idea for an innovative form of technology to address the issue.

	Meaning	Example Application
Conceptual/ Abstract thinking	Link content to themes and big ideas (e.g., conflict, cycles, patterns, interactions, systems). Apply principles and theories.	Apply a concept such as patterns by asking, "How does the decrease in the bee population affect patterns within other systems (agricultural, economic, other species, etc.)?"
Posing boundaries	Make a task more challenging by posing set criteria and constraints within the task (Stambaugh, 2018).	Develop a proposal that includes ways for farmers to decrease the use of pesticides while also increasing food yield.

Source: Republished with permission of Taylor and Francis, from *Collaboration, Coteaching, and Coaching in Gifted Education: Sharing Strategies to Support Gifted Learners*, Mofield, E., & Phelps, V. (2020), permission conveyed through Copyright Clearance Center, Inc.

Depth of Knowledge: A Path Towards Expertise

Webb's Depth of Knowledge (DOK) framework (1997) is a model that can be used to analyze cognitive demands required by standards, assessments, and assignments. In the context of applying "vertical differentiation," it provides a structure for thinking about increasing the cognitive expectations for students to engage in a task. Unlike Bloom's taxonomy which emphasizes analysis, evaluation, and synthesis as "high-level thinking," Webb's Depth of Knowledge focuses more on the mental processes the student must use to apply their learning and ultimately *transfer* their learning. Some have explained that Bloom's taxonomy, which was originally intended for organizing instructional objectives, focuses on verbs (create, analyze, defend), but Webb's Depth of Knowledge focuses on the level of cognitive complexity required to create, analyze, defend, etc. (Hess et al., 2009). The Depth of Knowledge (DOK) levels are also parallel to Hattie et al.'s (2017) Visible Learning organization of surface, deep, and transfer learning and provide a framework for teachers to develop complex task demands.

DOK Level 1 is basic recall and reproduction of information. Students recall, restate, and find facts, define terms, and list information. Though this is a basic level, students indeed need exposure and initial experiences in learning content. This level relates to surface learning as it provides a foundation for deeper learning.

DOK Level 2 is basic application of information. Students organize, summarize, infer, develop a main idea, write a paragraph, classify information, find relationships, and make connections with content. If you compare this to Bloom's taxonomy, you may notice that many "analysis" types of thinking belong here. At this level, students are demonstrating that they understand the content, how it is organized, and can apply their learning. When teachers ask students to organize information on a graphic organizer, students are often working at DOK Level 2. At this level, students are strengthening their schema and moving towards deep learning, especially as they understand how concepts relate to one another.

DOK Level 3 is strategic thinking. Beyond applying and organizing knowledge, at this level, students are required to strategically plan. They might plan how to defend an argument, justify a conclusion with reasoning, or make a decision. The tasks at this level might involve more than one response, and the cognitive demands are more abstract and complex. DOK 3 Level tasks require students to do more with the content than what is "right there"; students must apply reasoning and make decisions using what they know about the content. Critical thinking such as evaluating evidence, determining implications of a decision, verifying the reasonableness of evidence, and constructing valid arguments are often part of DOK Level 3 tasks. DOK Level 3 tasks might also involve nonroutine applications where students strategically apply knowledge in a new way (e.g., What if plants did not receive sunlight for one week, how would this affect the chloroplasts and its production of food?). Additionally, DOK 3 Level tasks might include connecting ideas with supporting evidence and analyzing interrelationships between ideas and concepts. In DOK 3 Level tasks, students are required to consolidate their learning from DOK 1 and 2 and make connections between concepts. Here, students are engaged in deep learning.

DOK Level 4 is extended thinking. This level requires students to take all of what they can do from DOK 1, 2, and 3 and to arrive at a large conclusion, justify conclusions from multiple resources, develop solutions for real-world problems, and/or transfer their learning to multiple contexts and conditions. This is ultimately what we as educators want our students to be able to do— apply "school learning" to the real world. If students learn about the water cycle, we want them to not just understand it, but to be able to use this knowledge in addressing sustainability in real-world environmental issues. These types of tasks usually involve an element of time. Often, students cannot complete these tasks within one lesson. Additionally, these tasks often include the use of multiple resources for students to arrive at a conclusion, restructure data, or develop a solution to a real-world issue. DOK Level 4 tasks reflect transfer learning because students extend their thinking by applying a deep understanding to solve problems and examine issues in other contexts.

Table 1.3 summarizes how Webb's Depth of Knowledge aligns with teaching practices, questions and prompts for student engagement, student

Table 1.3 Teaching and Learning with Webb's Depth of Knowledge

	Teaching Practices	Question Prompts	Student Learning (Processes)	Content and Tools
DOK 1	Provides for practice Demonstrates Models Defines	Who? What? When? Where? How? When?	Memorize Recall Restates	Vocabulary Facts Rules Visuals
DOK 2	Builds schema Teaches for conceptual understanding	Why? How is this the same? How is this different? What examples can you give? What leads to? How does this relate to __?	Compares Contrasts Estimates Makes inferences Explains relationships	Graphic Organizers Cause-effect Sequencing Explanatory writing Research to understand
DOK 3	Applies schema Promotes peer-to-peer dialogue Requires reasoning and evidence	Justify, explain why__. How would you decide __? How would you test__? Should___? Explain with reasoning. How are __, and __ interrelated? What if__? How would this change __?	Justifies Evaluates evidence Makes decisions Uses criteria Reasons with evidence Plans an argument Tests ideas Analyzes interrelationships	Debates Hypothesis testing Argument essay What if___ scenarios Number talks Analyzing primary sources for bias Research to conclude or justify
DOK 4	Applies schema to broader contexts Facilitates	Create a plan to __ Create a solution for __. Apply information from multiple sources to argue__ What other models might work? How might you adapt __ so that it is applicable to __?	Transfers knowledge to new contexts Synthesizes information from multiple sources to justify/conclude	Problem-based learning Developing solutions Arriving at large conclusions Planning experiments Research to produce or apply new ideas Make conclusions from multiple sources Multimedia products

Table 1.4 DOK Examples in Content Areas

	English Language Arts	Math	Social Studies	Science
DOK 1	Describe the conflict in the fable.	What is 40% of 120?	What is the 19th Amendment?	What are the parts of a plant cell?
DOK 2	What is the main outcome of the conflict?	Create a model to show 35% of 70.	What factors led to the 19th Amendment?	Create a Venn Diagram showing the similarities and differences between plant and animal cells.
DOK 3	Did the main character's internal conflict lead to his/her external conflict? Justify your answer with reasoning from the text.	Complete the following word sentence using only digits less than 4 and without repeating a digit. ___ % of ___ = ___	Was the United States a democracy before the passing of the 19th Amendment? Develop an argument using supportive evidence.	What would happen if there were a change in homeostasis within the cell? Explain how this imbalance would affect various cell organelles and their interactions.
DOK 4	Does conflict lead to opportunity or to chaos? Support your response using this fable and two other fables.	What percent of a person's life is spent on "screen time?" Develop a plan to estimate your data and present your reasoning and conclusions to the class.	What types of social movements throughout American history and today are similar to the Women's suffrage movement? Use multiple sources to create a presentation to depict patterns of social justice and how these are relevant to issues of today.	How are plants affected by changing climate conditions? After researching the topic from multiple sources, create a model to explain how changes in the environment affect a cell's structure and function.

learning, and the type of content and tools that might be used to plan or assess instruction.

An analogy I often use to explain DOK levels includes how players learn to play football. DOK Level 1 includes learning the rules of the game and roles of various players. At DOK Level 2, players practice the various skills used in the game (e.g., throwing the ball, kicking the ball). At DOK Level 3, players play the game and reason through how to play the game against a particular type of opponent, thinking through various decisions about offense and defense plays. At DOK Level 4, players are equipped to transfer their skills in playing football to playing another sport with similar skills such as soccer. The analogy shows the learning and practice (DOK Levels 1 and 2) is intended to actually play the game (DOK Level 3), and the skills can transfer to other contexts (DOK Level 4). We should ask ourselves, "do students have opportunities to actually 'play the game' by applying what they learn or are they simply practicing skills over and over?" Table 1.4 shows examples of DOK levels in various content areas.

How can we make sure gifted students are not going through school friction-free? When planning instruction for gifted learners, the DOK framework can serve as a guide for increasing the cognitive demands when planning instructional tasks. With an intentional aim to provide more cognitive complexity and opportunities for students to grapple with advanced content, we can provide the friction needed for students to explore content deeply.

Thinking as an Expert: Knowing Why and What if?

In gifted education, attention is given to exposing students to methodologies and processes that experts use within their discipline to solve authentic problems (Beasley et al., 2017; Erickson, 2007; Phenix, 1964; Stambaugh & Mofield, 2022; Tomlinson, 2004). Experts think about problems and issues differently than novices. Particularly, they "develop mental frameworks for organizing knowledge, retrieve integrated collective facts (rather than piecemeal facts), perceive structures of situations in order to know next steps and examine patterns, and understand when to revise ideas" (Adams et al., 2008, para. 2). Because of their more sophisticated organization of knowledge, they have better strategies for accessing information and using it, and they employ better self-regulation skills (Chi et al., 1988). While novices can solve problems based only on what they have seen before, experts are able to transfer their learning and solve complex problems in new contexts, no longer depending on rules and facts, but on their extensive knowledge and experience.

How does this translate to instruction and differentiation for gifted learners? By focusing on incorporating DOK Level 3 and 4 (strategic thinking and extended thinking) with advanced content, students are introduced to contexts to think as experts. Though different discipline areas require specific structures and ways of thinking about the content, the skills such as evaluating interrelationships among concepts, making judgments based on specific criteria, developing logical arguments to support claims, and transferring learning to new contexts are all skills related to developing expertise.

These skills can be developed through the structuring and restructuring of mental models. Mental models are the mental representations (knowledge structures) of how ideas are related to one another (see Lekshmi, 2020). As students learn new concepts, these mental models are restructured and become more complex.

The strategies within this book pave the path for building these mental models as students explore how and why concepts of a discipline connect. Through understanding the "why" behind interrelationships, students deepen their conceptual understanding of the content. Also, by applying knowledge to "what if" situations (e.g., new contexts, new solution ideas, real-world applications), students have opportunities to practice applying methodologies related to a discipline. The big idea is this: when students understand the structure of a system within a discipline, this system can be changed to produce a desired outcome, new idea, or solution.

The talent development model of gifted education (Subotnik et al., 2011) emphasizes the development of domain-specific abilities to move students on trajectories towards developing expertise. The strategies provided in this book can be used to scaffold students towards their next stages in this trajectory. These strategies prepare students to practice "thinking and doing as an expert" by developing strong mental models of the concepts they are learning. Though these strategies are not necessarily specific to content areas, they provide general approaches for building and supporting strong mental structures in any content area because they emphasize how concepts connect and then transfer to new contexts. [See Stambaugh and Mofield (2022) for content-specific models used to deliberately cultivate expert-like thinking].

Table 1.5 notes differences between novices and experts in regard to their organization of knowledge, approaches to problem solving, and use of metacognition. It also shows instructional strategies that can be used to support the progression from novice learning to expert-like thinking. Of course, gifted students in K-12 have likely not reached a level of expertise in any content area. However, in considering the aims of talent development, we can use this information to intentionally design instruction and use strategies to advance students towards their next levels of learning.

Steps
to conjugation)
cognates

Table 1.5 Instructional Approaches to Support Novice to Expert Learning

Characteristics of a Novice	Characteristics of an Expert	Instructional Strategies
Novices depend on rules and facts with little background knowledge or experience. Novices have difficulty making connections to previously learned content.	Experts have organized and integrated learning structures based on their knowledge base and experience.	Provide opportunities for students to make connections to previously learned material. Provide opportunities for students to understand the structure and organization of content (e.g., mind maps, graphic organizers) and develop their own structure for organizing content.
Novices spend time memorizing and recalling piecemeal facts. Information is stored in "silos."	Experts think about knowledge organized around core concepts and principles.	Include essential questions, links to big ideas, and emphasis on thematic connections.
Novices have difficulty perceiving the big picture or have only a superficial understanding of the problem.	Experts solve problems by creating mental representations of the problem and explore the nuances, complexities, and root of the problem.	Provide opportunities for students to examine the relationships and complexities of a problem (e.g., implications, assumptions, points of view). Provide opportunities for students to make connections between and across content.

(Continued)

Table 1.5 (Continued)

Characteristics of a Novice	Characteristics of an Expert	Instructional Strategies
Novices depend on following formulas, routines, and rules for solving problems, slowing down the problem-solving process. Novices do not see patterns and have difficulty distinguishing between relevant and irrelevant information. They ask questions about procedures.	Experts have superior working memory and can retrieve information with little attention or effort. Because of experience, they can solve problems in multiple contexts and discern between relevant and irrelevant information. They ask questions about concepts for deep understanding.	Provide various contexts for students to retrieve information in multiple ways and from various perspectives (e.g., Schema Board, Metaphorical Connections, Synectics, Six Thinking Hats). *? What ?* Help students discriminate between relevant and irrelevant information and provide non-routine applications of learning (DOK Level 3). Scaffold to decrease the demands of cognitive load (from following rules/procedures) so students can more readily retrieve information.
Novices are not aware of their thinking patterns and cannot detect why decisions were flawed. They are unaware of what they do not know.	Experts employ sophisticated metacognition (self-regulated learning) and ask questions based on what they need to know. They understand why they fail and how to redirect their efforts.	Purposefully embed metacognitive and meta-affective strategies so that students are more aware of their thinking processes. Explicitly guide students to think about why something did not work and next steps.

Content adapted from Chi et al. (1988); Persky and Robinson (2017)

Essentially, experts see the whole of parts working together. They (1) understand the basic concepts of their discipline and think about how these concepts relate to one another in an organized structure, (2) internalize the underlying structural pattern of concepts and apply them to novel contexts (Bransford et al., 2000; Stern et al., 2021), and (3) transfer these generalized

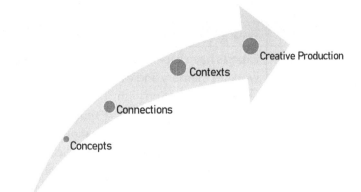

Figure 1.3 Expertise Thinking: Concepts to Creative Production

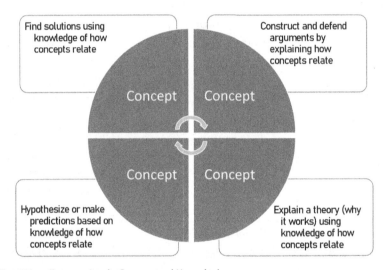

Figure 1.4 Four Ways Experts Apply Conceptual Knowledge

principles to solving problems and creating new knowledge, thereby making new contributions to a field. Figure 1.3 illustrates this progression from knowing concepts, connecting concepts, applying this knowledge to new contexts and situations, and creating new ideas.

Experts apply their understanding of conceptual relationships in a number of ways. Figure 1.4 illustrates that experts find solutions, defend arguments, make hypotheses or predictions, and explain theories based on their deep understanding of the patterns and relationships between concepts (Stern et al., 2021).

Teaching Students to Think as Experts: What, Why, What if?

You might be thinking, *"This sounds great, but how does this apply to teaching third graders? They're not exactly 'experts' yet."* Indeed. But, they can be exposed to the core conceptual understanding of a discipline early on. In the chapters that follow, I aim to provide concrete strategies to guide students on a path towards creative production. Specifically, students can understand the underlying structure of how concepts are connected, consider other contexts for application, and use conceptual understanding to develop creative solutions or new ideas.

To simplify this, I have developed a short rhyme for creating tasks that elicit students to construct knowledge as experts do. This is something I have written on a sticky note next to my desk as I write curriculum materials.

Good idea!

Justify, explain why.

Show how x relates to y.

Evaluate.

See points of view.

Create a plan or something new.

To help students construct knowledge like experts

This short rhyme is structured through a pyramid to reflect planning for students to know, relate, and extend their learning (see Figure 1.5). The bottom of the inverted pyramid represents the knowledge or concepts (the "what") students need to learn. Moving upward, the middle emphasizes that students explore relationships and "why" (e.g., why did you arrive at this conclusion? Explain why x causes y). When students evaluate and "justify and explain why," they are supporting a conclusion with reasoning and evidence, defending arguments by articulating how concepts are connected, and explaining why the facts are what they are.. Showing how x relates to y emphasizes

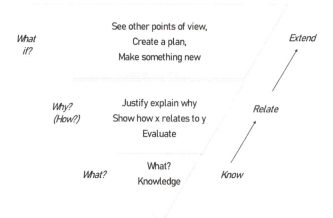

Figure 1.5 Know-Relate-Extend: What, Why, and What if Thinking

the examination of relationships between concepts, and this becomes more complex as students examine interrelationships between *multiple* concepts. At the top part of the pyramid, the emphasis is on creative thinking: using imagination, thinking through hypothetical situations, analyzing alternative explanations, and modifying existing ideas to make new ideas. Creating a plan or something new allows for students to strategically apply knowledge in a new way. This is the largest and broadest area of the pyramid representing the openness of these types of prompts and broad applications (transfer).

This rhyme suggests the heart of moving students towards expert-like thinking by prompting them to think *why* and *what if?* Through understanding "why" relationships and systems are what they are, students strengthen their schema and deepen their understanding of the content. In applying knowledge to "what if" situations (e.g., new contexts, new solution ideas, real-world applications), students transfer content to other contexts.

The strategies found in Chapters 3–7 fit within the "why" and "what if" thinking dimensions, aimed to move students into DOK Levels 3 and 4 (deep learning and transfer learning). Table 1.6 provides an overview of how the strategies in the following chapters fit within this structure along with specific

Table 1.6 Strategies and Thinking Prompts for Relating and Extending Thinking

Quick Reference		Strategies	Thinking Prompts
Why?/How? (Relate)	Justify, explain why	• Argument Construction Model • Iceberg of Why's • Balloon Debate	• Debate ____ • Should___? • What is the underlying issue and why? • Use Elements of Thought to justify___
	Show how x relates to y	• Connections Web • Schema Board • Inductive reasoning • Synectic Analogies • Forced Associations • Metapatterns	• How do__,__, and ___ interrelate? • How does ___ contribute to__? • How does understanding this relationship provide new insight on __?
	Evaluate	• SWOT • Should-Could-Would criteria	• What criteria should be considered? • Which is better? Why?

(Continued)

Table 1.6 (Continued)

7 7

Quick Reference		Strategies	Thinking Prompts
What if? (Extend)	See points of view	• Six Thinking Hats • POWER Analysis • Argument Construction Models • Synectic Analogies	• What are the assumptions and implications of these points of view? • What if these points of view were considered? • How is ___ like___ and how is it not like__?
	Create a plan or something new	• SCAMPER Stretch • Synectic Triggers • Cascade of Consequences	• How might you modify__ to improve___? • What are the short and long-term consequences of___? • What if this is applied in other contexts? • What would happen if. . . ?

prompts to elicit student thinking. This model is revisited in Chapter 9 to illustrate how it can be used to tier student tasks with increased levels of complexity.

"Would, Could, Should" Litmus Test Reframed

If you have been in gifted education for a while, you are likely familiar with the litmus test for determining if curriculum is adequately differentiated for the gifted. Harry Passow (1982) provided an elegant three question test: "Would all children want to be involved in such learning experiences? Could all children participate in such learning experiences? Should all children be expected to succeed in such learning experiences?" If the answer is "yes" to any question, this suggests the learning experience may not be sufficiently challenging for gifted students.

This test has guided my own thinking for many years for creating complex tasks that match the readiness levels of gifted students. Through the traditional differentiation lens, these questions lead teachers to focus on developing increasingly complex tasks. However, in the context of talent development, these questions can be reframed as we consider how to plan instruction to spot and develop talent among a broader population of students, including students who are twice-exceptional and students from diverse backgrounds. The talent development view of giftedness adopts the idea that giftedness is dynamic, malleable, and shaped by external factors with a focus on identifying potential to be nurtured into achievement. Through this lens, I see vertical differentiation as a means to uncover potential in students and provide opportunities for students to "show and grow" their gifts and talents. I often like to say, "curriculum is opportunity that grows ability!"

Through a talent development lens, these questions can be reframed to provide opportunities for students (who may not be formally identified as gifted) to access high-level content:

1. Would the exposure to high-level content and challenge lead to next steps in talent development?
2. Could providing challenging learning experiences uncover potential?
3. What should we do to promote access to high-level content and challenging learning experiences?

If we plan instruction so that the answer is "Yes" to 1 and 2, and if we have many ideas for answering number 3, then we are more likely to identify and cultivate talent in more students. Many students benefit from tasks that demand cognitive rigor, though sometimes supports and scaffolds are needed to promote this access. Therefore, I'll repeat what I stated at the beginning of this chapter—these strategies are not reserved to be used only with gifted students, though you may find it necessary to vary the complexity and amount of scaffolding to support students with various readiness levels. When we plan instruction and respond to these reframed questions with "Yes! Exposure to high-level content will lead to the cultivation of talent! Yes, these challenging experiences will uncover potential! We will support students in accessing high-level content!" then we are opening doors and opportunities for students to develop potential into realized talents!

2

The Big Picture

Frameworks for Thinking

In the chapters that follow, I provide specific strategies for developing skills to "think like an expert" through critical, creative, and analytical thinking integrated with content. The strategies focus on analyzing relationships, defending ideas, evaluating ideas, solving problems, and transferring learning to new contexts. Before diving into these specific concrete strategies, it is important to see the larger picture of where these skills fit in the context of familiar frameworks and curriculum design for deep learning. While I believe strategies are important, having a deeper understanding of frameworks allows teachers to make better instructional decisions.

This chapter provides an overview of building conceptual understanding and critical and creative thinking models, setting the context for understanding why these strategies support the development of expertise. I conclude the chapter with an introduction to Stretch Prompts which can be used as a quick reference for planning vertical differentiation, stretching students to apply thinking to more complex cognitive demands.

Learning Goals

When planning for vertical differentiation within a lesson, we must first consider what students need to know, understand, and do (think) in the lesson.

DOI: 10.4324/9781003293286-3

[handwritten: Basics]

[handwritten: Grammar / Vocab]

Knowledge Goals

According to the Understanding by Design framework (McTighe & Wiggins, 2012), knowledge goals include the facts, terms, people, definitions, rules, and other content-based ideas students will acquire. Because vertical differentiation emphasizes teaching for the development of expertise, it is important to note that experts know a large amount of facts and information, but they know them in the context of a larger conceptual framework (Persky & Robinson, 2017). In terms of challenging gifted students, knowledge goals might include content from above-grade level standards (remember A is for Advance the Content) or content that allows students to engage in a more in-depth exploration of facts and issues. Knowledge goals focus on developing surface learning (initial understanding of concepts) to set the stage for deeper learning.

Understanding Goals

[handwritten: Last beyond the lesson]

Understanding goals link directly to the principles, overarching ideas, essential understandings, and generalizations of the content. Understanding goals are understandings of the discipline that last well beyond the lesson (enduring understandings). Any vertical adjustment to content or processing skills should ultimately support how the student will better understand the essential understandings of the lesson (see Conceptual Thinking in this chapter). These conceptual understandings and principles develop as students make connections across various concepts and engage in deep learning.

Process "Do" Goals

[handwritten: What is done in "brain" to achieve Knowledge / Understanding / Teach me something]

Process (or "Do") goals include the thinking, procedural, or discipline-specific skills students use in their learning. These goals are what students do in their heads and serve as an "intellectual avenue" (Doubet & Hockett, 2015, p. 40) for achieving the knowledge goals and understanding goals. In the context of vertical differentiation for gifted students, these goals should incorporate high-level processing, with an emphasis on incorporating DOK 3 and DOK 4 level learning. Additionally, specific critical and creative thinking objectives fit within these process goals (see taxonomies for critical and creative thinking in this chapter).

These three types of goals link together and overlap to achieve the ultimate outcome of deep learning and transfer. Doubet and Hockett (2015) succinctly explain, "We want students to use what they *know* and can *do* to show what they *understand*" (p. 42). Table 2.1 provides an overview for applying McTighe and Wiggins's (2012) Understanding by Design to vertical differentiation (differentiating "up").

Table 2.1 Planning for Knowledge, Understand, and Do Goals with Vertical Differentiation

Know	Understand	Do (Process)
• Above Grade-level standards • More in-depth investigation of facts, evidence, and issues	• Concept-based connections, theories, principles, and generalizations (conceptual "velcro") • Essential understandings and questions	• High-level thinking skills (see models for critical and creative thinking; DOK Level 3 and DOK Level 4) • Discipline-specific literacy (thinking, writing, and arguing like a scientist, etc.) • Metacognition skills
Example: Students will know persuasive techniques: appeal to reason, appeal to emotion, appeal to authority, rhetorical questions.	Example: Students will understand *that* language can change a person's point of view.	Example: Students will justify the most effective persuasive technique for a given purpose and audience.

Conceptual Thinking: Big Ideas (Understand Goals)

It has been said that concepts are the building blocks of expertise (Erickson, 2007). Not only do experts know core concepts of their discipline, but experts also understand how concepts connect. As discussed in Chapter 1, experts organize their thinking around core ideas, concepts, or principles as opposed to a list of facts. Though it is important for students to learn facts and content information (knowledge goals), to achieve transfer of learning to new contexts and real-world applications students must understand how broad concepts, principles, and generalizations tie the content together. As we design learning experiences, we must ask ourselves "What will endure? What will be worth knowing and learning long after this lesson has taken place?" This is the "so what" of the lesson, the very core of what we want students to understand deeply.

To guide students to see these big picture ideas, we must intentionally plan learning goals that pave the way for deep understanding of content. For example, in a unit on ancient civilizations an understanding goal might be centered around the concepts of culture and progress: students will understand that *progress is defined by culture and point* of view (a tip is to include the word 'that' in front of the big idea students will understand). For math: students will understand that *multiplication is another way to perform addition.*

Include "THAT" in front of Big learning ideas

Students need to Arrive @ Big idea understandings NOT be told

It is <u>important</u>, however, for *students* themselves to <u>arrive at these</u> big idea <u>understandings, not for the teacher to outright tell students</u> in a lesson. In some of the strategies that follow (e.g., Connections Web, Inductive Reasoning: Group, Regroup, Here's the Scoop, Chapter 3), students have the opportunity to develop their own big idea statements.

When instruction is planned with an understanding goal in mind, the content is then "integrated." Students can see patterns of how ideas are connected at a conceptual level; thus, they are able to transfer learning more easily across contexts. For example, by understanding that *progress is defined by culture and point of view*, this enduring understanding applies not only to ancient civilizations, but also transfers to modern living such as the impact of globalization on culture. The <u>curriculum becomes integrated when students see the connections</u> within and <u>across disciplines</u> (Hockett & Brighton, 2016). This integration allows for breadth in the curriculum where students' learning extends to other content areas or real-world situations, well-suited for planning DOK 4 Level tasks.

Planning With Big Ideas

You can use a number of approaches for planning instruction around big ideas. One way is to design lessons and units around big ideas or concepts. This idea is popular in gifted education curriculum (e.g., William and Mary units, Vanderbilt PTY units, CLEAR curriculum series) as it brings coherence to a curriculum by connecting lessons together with a "conceptual velcro." <u>Concepts can be</u> universal (e.g., patterns, systems, change) that <u>apply across disciplines,</u> or they <u>might be specific to a content area</u> (e.g., supply and demand in Social Studies; probability in Mathematics). Teachers can design curriculum to ask students to make connections to concept generalizations throughout a unit, guiding students to see patterns and link their learning to a large structure (Stambaugh & Mofield, 2022). For example, in a unit structured around the idea of "patterns" with the generalization "patterns allow for prediction," the teacher might ask <u>"how do patterns allow for prediction in the story we read?"</u> To make this thinking visible, concept word walls or maps (McTighe & Silver, 2020; Stambaugh & Mofield, 2022) can be constructed to display these connections. Major concepts, generalizations, and/or principles related to a unit can be recorded on a board or chart paper so that throughout a unit students can explain connections they are making from facts, details, evidence, quotes, and definitions. These concepts and generalizations should be visible throughout the unit so that students can continually support these big ideas with new learning.

Essential Questions

Lessons can also be designed around essential questions that elicit open-ended responses around concepts and ideas rather than isolated facts (McTighe &

Wiggins, 2013). The answers to the essential questions lead to enduring understandings. For example, an essential question might be "How does the structure of a plant influence its function?" or "How are resources distributed in a society? Is this fair?" Essential questions can be explored over time in multiple lessons and units, which allow for transferable learning and deep understanding. McTighe and Wiggins (2013) explain that essential questions help students make sense of facts and knowledge and should be thought-provoking, lead to new questions, and should capture the "core" of what students should be learning about the discipline. These, like the concept word wall, should be visible to students, and student responses should be supported with logical reasoning and evidence (eliciting DOK Level 3 responses).

Topic: A Study In

Another way to build in a transfer of learning is to use the prompt "Topic: A study in____" (Silver & Perini, 2010) to frame conceptual understanding around a unit. For example, a unit about persuasion through using rhetorical devices in speeches might be framed as "Rhetoric: A study in interactions" because learners understand how various parts of a speech (purpose, claim, logos, ethos, pathos, evidence) interact to persuade an audience. You may ask students directly, "What is this topic a study in?" and require students to respond with a justifiable response: "I see topic as a study in concept because____." Students can be provided with a list of concept words (e.g., change, cycles, organization, patterns; see Figure 2.1) to justify their responses. For example, in studying about the scientific method, a student might respond, "I see the scientific method as a study in design because various designs lead to different conclusions about the data. How you design an experiment will affect the conclusions made," while another student might respond with "I see the scientific method as a study in cycles because when the science experiment is complete, it is not really complete; it leads to new questions and new hypotheses to be tested." Though not exhaustive, Figure 2.1 includes a list of concepts that are applicable across content areas. Many of these are ideas from Mortimer Adler's volumes of the *Syntopicon*, a collection of enduring ideas.

Concept Relationships

How do we move students from merely identifying concepts to transferring these concepts to other contexts? First, students must identify and understand the concepts presented within a unit and understand the relationships between them. For example, students might examine the concepts of patterns, structure, and meaning within a poem. Then, students examine the relationships among these concepts by answering essential questions that connect them (e.g., How do patterns impact the overall structure? How do patterns

Adaptation	Function	Perseverance
Beauty*	Growth	Progress*
Cause and Effect*	Hypothesis*	Quality*
Change*	Interactions	Quantity*
Chaos and Order	Language*	Relationships
Correlation	Necessity*	Revolution*
Cycles	Organization	Sign and Symbol*
Design	One and Many*	Structure and Parts
Evolution*	Part and Whole	Systems
Experience*	Patterns	
Form*	Power	

Figure 2.1 Sample List of Concepts

Source: *from Adler, M., & Gorman, W. (1990). The great ideas: A syntopicon of great books of the Western world (Volumes I-III). Encyclopedia Britannica.

and structure develop the meaning in the poem?). As students engage with content, they can arrive at conclusions to answer these questions and examine how the big idea "structure promotes meaning" transfers to other poems and genres of literature.

Though the rest of this book provides specific strategies for developing meaningful, engaging instruction and tasks that challenge high-potential and gifted learners, it is important not to overlook the big picture of pre-planning the integration of transferable concepts in the overall design of a lesson or unit. I would caution to not use the strategies that follow as "add-ons" to lessons and activities. Rather, they should be considered as a *means* for students to achieve learning goals tied directly to content and conceptual understanding, centered around thought-provoking essential questions that lead to enduring understandings.

Models for Critical and Creative Thinking (Process/"Do" Goals)

The strategies in the coming chapters are organized by cognitive demand (strategies for analysis, understanding the problem, etc.). These strategies include both critical and creative thinking, and so, I have refrained from organizing the strategies as creative strategies vs. critical thinking strategies because they so often overlap. For example, before applying creative divergent thinking to developing a solution, critical thinking is needed to analyze the problem and later evaluate the solution against set criteria. When analyzing how parts of a system interact (e.g., ecosystem, elements of a story, parts of government), this involves critical thinking in analyzing the relationships between the parts and also creative thinking in posing new insight about those relationships.

Throughout this book, you will see elements of both critical and creative thinking within the strategies. Specifically, Paul and Elder's (2019) Model (Elements of Thought) is embedded as critical thinking and Torrance's (1962) fluency, flexibility, originality, and elaboration are applied as creative thinking. Though these are common models in gifted education, I provide an overview here to show the foundation for forthcoming strategies and to provide a base for readers who may need an introduction to these models.

Critical Thinking

Critical thinking involves using reasoning and logic to analyze, evaluate, and construct arguments. Many of the strategies in Chapter 7 address the skill of argument construction, while many of the creative problem-solving strategies in Chapter 5 involve evaluation criteria for ideas. These thinking skills and processes can be embedded within a process ("do") goal, leading students to justify, evaluate, and make inferences about the essential understandings.

Cambridge's Assessment Taxonomy of Critical Thinking Skills and Processes identifies a number of critical thinking processes:

- ◆ Analysis—dissect arguments, differentiating relevant from irrelevant information, identifying unstated assumptions
- ◆ Evaluation—judge the relevance, sufficiency, significance, and credibility of arguments. Assessing the soundness of reasoning within an argument
- ◆ Inference—consider point of view, claims, principles, and implications of a claim
- ◆ Construction—take arguments further, respond to dilemmas, justify decisions
- ◆ Self-reflection—evaluate one's own reasoning; question one's preconceptions (Black et al., 2008, p. 32)

This taxonomy may be useful to teachers in crafting critical thinking goals tied to content. For example, a science teacher might use this framework to create a lesson goal such as "students will assess the soundness of reasoning for arguments for and against using corn as a biofuel."

Paul and Elder's Elements of Thought and Intellectual Standards

Paul and Elder's (2019) Model of Critical Thinking includes eight Elements of Thought that can apply to thinking about decisions, content, and issues. These elements can be integrated into debates, creative problem solving, reflections, Socratic Seminars, simulations, and other in-class activities (See also Little, 2001). You will see how many strategies in the chapters that follow naturally fit with this model (see Balloon debates, SWOT, etc.). These Elements of Thought are also identifiable within the Cambridge Critical Thinking Skills and Processes Taxonomy previously described.

Elements of Thought:

◆ Purpose—What is the purpose of examining this content, problem, or issue?
◆ Question—What is the overall question I am seeking to answer?
◆ Assumptions—What underlying assumptions shape my thinking about___?
◆ Point of View—What point of view is applied here? What other points of view are important to consider?
◆ Data—What evidence supports my reasoning?
◆ Concepts—What concepts or ideas are important in understanding and thinking about___?
◆ Inferences—What conclusions can I make from this data?
◆ Implications/Consequences—What are the implications and consequences of ___?

These questions can apply to any issue, text, or media eliciting opportunities for students to arrive at and support sound conclusions. Paul and Elder (2019) explain that these Elements of Thought do not work in isolation; rather, they are all integrated and overlap as students reason through an issue. For example, when examining the question "Should we ban genetically modified foods?" this can be viewed from a point of view, for a purpose, and through various assumptions. This model for reasoning is excellent for discussing essential questions in a unit and debatable issues. Additionally, students can build arguments based on these elements (see Chapter 7, Argument Construction Model).

In addition to these Elements of Thought, Paul and Elder describe nine Intellectual Standards which can be used to judge one's strength of reasoning. Critical thinkers think about their own thinking with questions around these nine standards.

Intellectual Standards:

◆ Clarity—Is this reasoning clear? Is elaboration needed? Would it be helpful to provide another example or express differently?
◆ Accuracy—Is this true? How can we know this is accurate?
◆ Precision—Are enough details provided? How can you be more specific?

- Relevance—Is this directly tied to what we need to know? Is this related to the question we are asking?
- Depth—Are the complexities of the issue addressed or is this just superficial reasoning? Have we explored beneath the surface of the issue or problem?
- Breadth—How else might we look at this issue? What other points of view should be considered?
- Logic—Is this making sense? Is the inference connected to the evidence? Do the thoughts support each other?
- Significance—What is the most important information? Which of these ideas/facts/questions is most important?
- Fairness—Am I making unfair assumptions? Am I distorting the use of evidence and concepts? Are my conclusions justifiable?

These Intellectual Standards overlap with the Elements of Thought and can be taught to students to critically evaluate the strength of their own reasoning. For example, how *clear* is my *purpose*? Is the *evidence relevant* to the *question*? Have I considered the most important (*significant*) *implications* and *consequences*? The construction of well-reasoned judgments and other objectives can be supported by the intentional use of these Intellectual Standards.

Creative Thinking

Creative thinking involves looking at problems with new perspectives with an aim to create something new. Kettler et al. (2018) have developed a taxonomy of creative thinking that can apply across various content domains (see Table 2.2). This taxonomy delineates creative thinking through five areas and 16 student expectations. These expectations can be used to articulate and plan instructional sequences for embedding creative thinking within math, language arts, social studies, and science. This taxonomy can also serve as a guide for developing process ("do") goals within lesson planning for vertical differentiation.

Dimensions of Creativity

The four dimensions of creativity are processes used to develop divergent thinking. These include the following (Guilford, 1967; Torrance, 1962):

- Fluency refers to the quantity of ideas, solutions, or possible answers regardless of quality (originality or elaboration).
- Flexibility refers to diverse ideas, including those from various points of view. Flexibility can refer to finding connections between seemingly unrelated ideas.

Table 2.2 Taxonomy of Creative Thinking

I. Idea generation	1.1: Students will generate ideas that reflect original thinking about the content of study.
	1.2: Students will effectively use a wide range of idea creation techniques.
	1.3: Students will communicate clearly the ideas that they develop.
	1.4: Students will develop alternative explanations for events or phenomena within the content of study.
	1.5: Students will construct theories to explain phenomena within the content of study.
2. Idea elaboration	2.1: Students will elaborate their own ideas as well as the ideas of others by adding more details.
	2.2: Students will analyze and refine their own ideas as well as the ideas of others to make ideas more accurate or effective.
	2.3: Students will analyze and evaluate alternative explanations or alternative points of view.
3. Idea connections	3.1: Students will make connections between new ideas and existing ideas as well as between multiple existing ideas.
	3.2: Students will combine parts of existing ideas to generate original extensions of those ideas.
4. Problem Solving	4.1: Students will recognize and describe problems that could be solved.
	4.2: Students will apply problem-solving protocols to generate creative solutions to problems.
	4.3: Students will predict outcomes in hypothetical models.
5. Original work	5.1: Students will produce products that reflect originality and are authentic to the domain of study.
	5.2: Students will use technology to generate innovative outcomes within the domain of study.
	5.3: Students will demonstrate originality, imagination, and innovative thinking in their work within the unit of study.

- ◆ Originality refers to unique, uncommon, and unusual ideas. This might include unusual combinations or modifications of ideas.
- ◆ Elaboration refers to adding details and explanations to clearly articulate ideas. It refers to the quality of expression of ideas (not too much or too little).

These four dimensions of creativity are illuminated within Kettler et al.'s Taxonomy of Creativity. These dimensions provide a structure for teachers to teach creative thinking and also observe and assess creativity in student work. Many of the strategies in this book can be used to elicit divergent thinking through the creative dimensions. For example, the Wonder Window (see Chapter 3) prompts students to develop several questions around a topic (fluency—idea generation) while the Synectic strategies (see Chapter 6) enhance idea connections by encouraging students to think with flexibility as they understand a concept or topic more deeply.

Combining Taxonomies: Creativity and Critical Thinking Matrix

Creativity involves the "generation of (a) high-quality ideas or products that are both (b) novel and (c) useful/appropriate within the context of the task" (Kettler et al., 2018, p. 18). In considering this definition, it is important to recognize the role of critical thinking in evaluating the meaning of "high-quality," "novelty," and "usefulness." For example, an individual advocating for a new creative solution or invention must communicate its usefulness effectively through reasoned arguments. Creative ideas are judged for their feasibility and relevance, and their implications should be considered from multiple points of view. This led me to the idea of merging the taxonomies into The Combined Critical and Creative Thinking Matrix. In Table 2.3, a few examples of combined creative and critical thinking skills are provided within each box, though other specific skill combinations from each taxonomy can also be applied.

Stretch Prompts

In this and the previous chapter, I have provided an overview for several models of thinking. These models are the backbone of creating deep learning experiences for students, but what does this really look like in day-to-day teaching? How do we actually develop and design tasks that emphasize extended thinking and transfer? How can we introduce students to construct knowledge as experts do?

Here, I introduce the use of Stretch Prompts to plan for vertical differentiation. Resource 2.1 shows them as basic prompts while Resource 2.2 provides

Table 2.3 The Combined Creativity and Critical Thinking Matrix

	Idea Generation	Idea Elaboration	Idea Connections	Problem Solving	Original Work
Analysis	Recognize an argument and develop alternative explanations for this argument.	Clarify meaning by elaborating with sufficient details.	Recognize the various types of reasoning for connecting various ideas.	Identify unstated assumptions within a defined problem.	Produce original products, clarifying meaning for its purpose and need within a domain.
Evaluation	Judge the credibility of an alternative explanation.	Judge the relevance and sufficiency of details and explanations.	Judge the significance of the connections between new and existing ideas.	Detect errors in proposing creative solutions for defined problems.	Assess the relevance, plausibility, and credibility of one's innovative idea.
Inference	Consider implications of constructed theories.	Elaborate on evidence, points of view, implications, and principles of the idea.	Consider the implications of combined ideas.	Predict outcomes in hypothetical models based on reason and evidence.	Develop an original product, considering its implications for various points of view.
Construction	Construct an argument for supporting new ideas or constructed theories.	Take an argument further with sufficient elaboration.	Formulate reasoned judgments for combining ideas.	Make rational decisions for applying creative solutions to a defined problem.	Construct an argument for the usefulness of an innovative idea.
Self-Reflection	Reflect on the process of idea generation.	Reflect on the effectiveness of elaboration.	Reflect on how original extensions of ideas emerged.	Reflect on one's preconceptions of the problem and proposed solutions.	Reflect on the creative process applied to original innovation.

Source: Based on Cambridge Assessment Taxonomy of Critical Thinking Skills and Processes (Black et al., 2008) and the Taxonomy for Creative Thinking (Kettler et al., 2018).

sentence frames to support students in developing responses (These are downloadable at www.routledge.com/9781032275581). As you review these prompts, consider how you might already incorporate analysis, critical thinking, debate, and other high-level questions within your lessons (questions on the left). Each Stretch Prompt adds a next step "stretch" to increase the cognitive demand (questions on the right). The stretch provides an opportunity for students to synthesize their learning by perceiving the "whole" of the parts, justifying their conclusions, improving ideas, or applying learning to other contexts. In most cases, these prompts show how a DOK Level 2 is stretched to a DOK Level 3. Note that DOK Level 4 tasks require more than a "strategy" within a lesson plan; DOK Level 4 tasks might involve a combination of many learning experiences. Remember, DOK Level 4 tasks often require multiple resources and multiple days to complete (Chapter 9, Planning for Deep Learning and Differentiation, provides examples of DOK Level 4 tasks using strategies in this book).

These Stretch Prompts are the foundation for the structure of this book. The chapters that follow provide more concrete applications of using these prompts. Each question on the left shows a basic way to apply initial surface learning. On the right, the prompt increases the complexity to require more strategic reasoning and elicit deeper learning. As you read over these explanations, keep in mind that they align to cultivate "thinking like an expert." They include an emphasis on analyzing complex relationships, understanding and synthesizing patterns, attending to relevant vs. irrelevant information, asking next step questions, and being aware of one's own thought processes.

1. Analysis—The analysis prompt supports students' development of schema as they examine the parts and structure of a topic. Students move into deeper learning as they examine the interrelationships of parts and apply nonroutine thinking as they think through "what if" questions if parts were changed or removed (Stambaugh & Mofield, 2022). Schema is strengthened as students justify these relationships with supporting evidence. Because students perceive the structure of how concepts are related, they can move towards developing a generalization or big idea about the "whole" of the parts (See Chapter 3—Strategies for Analysis).

2. Problem Solving—The Problem Solving prompt initially asks students to determine multiple causes and effects of an issue. The stretch allows for students to think about underlying causes of causes and forecast effects of effects, including unintended consequences. Additionally, students strategically think through missing pieces, evaluating what is important and relevant to know for the situation or issue. (See Chapter 4—Strategies for Problem Solving: Understanding the Problem)

Stretch Prompts

Analysis

What are the parts of ___?
What is the overall structure?
How do parts relate to one another?

What happens if a part is removed? What generalization can we make based on how the parts interact?

Problem Solving

What are the causes and effects of
the problem/issue? What might happen if___?

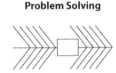

What are the causes of the causes? What are the effects of the effects?
What are unintended effects? What do we not know about the problem? What do we need to know in order to make a plan?

Creative Thinking for Solutions

What would need to be substituted, combined, adapted, modified,
put to another use, eliminated, or rearranged to create a solution for ___ or improve ____?

How have other problems like this been solved?
How might the idea/solution work in other contexts for other issues or problems?

Critical Thinking/ Decision-Making

What decisions need to be made about___?

What criteria can we use to make our decision? How can we make fair, logical decisions?

How is ___ like ___?
Explain at least three ways.

Metaphorical Thinking

How is ___ not like ___?
What new metaphor can you make?

What is the debatable issue?
What are various perspectives?
What evidence supports these perspectives?

Argument

How can the claim be supported by the known relationship of concepts?
What would strengthen the claim?
Are claims fair, logical, accurate, and supported with evidence?

How did I learn this?
Why did I learn it?
What was most difficult to do or understand?
How did new information confirm or contradict what I already know?

Metacognition

What adjustments need to be made?
What skills do I need in moving forward?
What do I do next?
What new questions do I have?

What are the main concepts?
How do they relate?
What's the big idea?
How do we see these concepts in our world?

Transfer

How does this apply to other contexts?
What is similar and different across the contexts?
How do experts think about and use this content?

Resource 2.1 Stretch Prompts without Frames

Identify and
Define 2 stretch prompts
Why relevant to learning

Stretch Prompts

What are the parts of ___?
What is the overall structure?
How do parts relate to one another?

_____ is made up of the smaller parts
such as_____
_____changes the structure.
_____ influences _____
_____relates to _____
_____changes_____

Analysis

What happens if a part is removed?
What generalization can we make
based on how the parts interact?

If _____is removed, then _____.
When ___ changes, we see its effect
on_____.

The big idea is _____.

What are the causes and effects of
the problem/issue? What might
happen if___?

_____, _____, and _____
cause the problem.
The effects of the problem
are_____, _____, and _____.

Problem Solving

What are the causes of the causes?
What are the effects of the effects?
What are unintended effects?
What do we not know about the
problem? What do we need to know
in order to make a plan?
___ caused the cause.
____ is an effect of this effect.
We still need to know_____.

What would need to be substituted,
combined, adapted, modified,
put to another use, eliminated, or
rearranged to create a solution for
___ or improve ____?

This could be improved by____.
We could try____.

Creative Thinking
for Solutions

How have other problems like this
been solved?
How might the idea/solution work
in other contexts for other issues
or problems?

When ____ happened, a solution
was to___.
We could use this idea____.
This can also work for____.

What decisions need to be made
about___?

We need to decide if___
Who___? What___?
When___? How___?

Critical Thinking/
Decision-Making

What criteria can we use to make
our decision? How can we make
fair, logical decisions?

Is it____?
To what extent does it__?
What impact will ___ have on___?
We know we accomplish the goal
when___.

How is ___ like ____?
Explain at least three ways

___ is like___because
Reason 1_____
Reason 2_____
Reason 3_____

Metaphorical Thinking

How is ___not like___?
What new metaphor can you make?

_____ is not like_____ because____.

_____ is like_____ because____.

What is the debatable issue?
What are various perspectives?
What evidence supports these perspectives?

Should_____? Is _____ or _____ better?
_____ would think____because_____.
___ supports the idea_____.

Argument

How can the claim be supported by the known relationship of concepts?
What would strengthen the claim?
Are claims fair, logical, accurate, and supported with evidence?

_____ is true because _____ interacts/ causes____.
We could improve this claim by_____.
The argument does not _____.
The argument is strong because____.

How did I learn this? Why did I learn it?
What was most difficult to do or understand?
How did new information confirm or contradict what I already know?

I was successful by_____.
This was important because_____.
The most difficult part was_____.
I already knew____.
I used to think___ now I know___.

Metacognition

What adjustments need to be made? What skills do I need in moving forward?
What do I do next?
What new questions do I have?

I still need _____.
Next, I will_____.
I still wonder about_____.

What are the main concepts?
How do they relate?
What's the big idea?
How do we see these concepts in our world?

The main concepts are___,___, and ____.
____ causes___.
____relates to_____.
We see this big idea_____.

Transfer

How does this apply to other contexts?
What is similar and different across the contexts?
How do experts think about and use this content?

In this context we see_____, but in this context _____.
An expert might ask_____.
An expert may use this to_____.

Resource 2.2 Stretch Prompts with Frames

3. Creative Thinking for Solutions—This prompt includes a well-known strategy, SCAMPER (Eberle, 2008), but takes it a step further when students think about how a problem might be solved by adapting ideas from other known solutions or considering how the new solution can also be adapted and transferred to other contexts. For example, if students think of a solution to convert ocean trash into a form of fuel, then this can also apply to a new idea of converting everyday household trash directly into a fuel source for the home. (See Chapter 5— Strategies for Problem-Solving: Creating and Evaluating Solutions)

4. Critical Thinking/Decision-Making—Critical thinking involves decision-making. Students are engaged in strategic thinking as they consider the questions to be asked in making a decision. The stretch is added when students select, develop, and test criteria to make their judgments. Students might consider feasibility, impact, and how developed criteria relates to the overall goal. (See Chapter 6— Strategies for Creating and Evaluating Solutions)

5. Metaphorical Thinking—The Metaphorical Thinking allows students to make connections between a familiar situation, object, or experience to content they are learning (the unfamiliar). As students connect their ideas, they support their reasoning with evidence. Then, the stretch applies when students consider other nuances in how the concept is *not* like the object and/or students create a new metaphor. Metaphorical Thinking can facilitate the development of more sophisticated mental models as students learn new content by connecting it to prior knowledge. (See Chapter 6—Strategies for Creative Thinking: Making Connections)

6. Argument—Debates are a natural fit with DOK Level 3. When students are asked to identify the debatable or ethical issues around a topic and then delve deep into the varied perspectives and evidence for each argument, they are engaged in assessing, justifying, and creating arguments. Student thinking is stretched when they are asked to justify their arguments by articulating how concepts relate to one another. Additionally, the added stretch elicits students to improve or critique claims and arguments. (See Chapter 7—Strategies for Constructing Arguments).

7. Metacognition—Metacognition involves bringing self-awareness to one's own thinking and learning. Experts use more metacognitive skills than novices and are aware of how they approach problems and how they think about them (see Persky & Robinson, 2017). Additionally, metacognition goes hand in hand with affective learning and

self-awareness. When students are asked "What was the most difficult to understand?" they can reflect on how they worked through the difficulty and can plan for next steps in their learning. Making decisions regarding resources and supports needed for further learning is a key part of strategic thinking. (See Chapter 8—Strategies for Metacognition).

8. Transfer—Transfer of learning is the ultimate outcome of education. Transfer occurs when students can apply their knowledge to new situations and contexts. This involves having a deep conceptual understanding of the big ideas or underlying principles of the content. Once students can identify how the major concepts of content relate, they can form generalizations (big ideas) that can be transferred to various contexts (Stern et al., 2021). Transfer is also enhanced when students can articulate how the big idea is applied similarly or differently to various contexts and situations. (See Big Idea Goals in this chapter and Chapter 9—Planning for Deep Learning)

These Stretch Prompts reflect various components of the thinking models previously described. They are designed to serve as a quick reference for planning vertically differentiated lessons and assignments as they provide opportunities to stretch students to engage more deeply with content with built-in tiers for extended learning, transfer, and reasoning. Not every prompt is applicable to all content areas, so it is important to consider which ones best fit the learning goals and standards for the lesson.

These prompts are not meant to be copied and distributed to students as a worksheet; rather, they should be carefully selected for guiding students to think about lesson content. For example, if using the Argument prompt, it is important to be prepared to help students relate the prompt to the content, with a debatable issue ready to identify and discuss. After students become familiar with the Stretch Prompts, you can cut them into strips, place in envelopes, and distribute to groups of students. When students select a card, the Stretch Prompt can serve as a tool for discussion starters, exit tickets, or class openers to review and extend content from the day before. Students could respond in writing to a prompt on their own paper, or students may use the prompts to focus small-group discussions, gallery walks, short formative assessments, or interactive notebooks. Figure 2.2 shows an example of laminated Stretch Prompts used for easy reference to add an additional level of cognitive demand during teaching.

The Stretch Prompts with sentence frames (Resource 2.2) support students in developing written or oral responses to these prompts, especially for

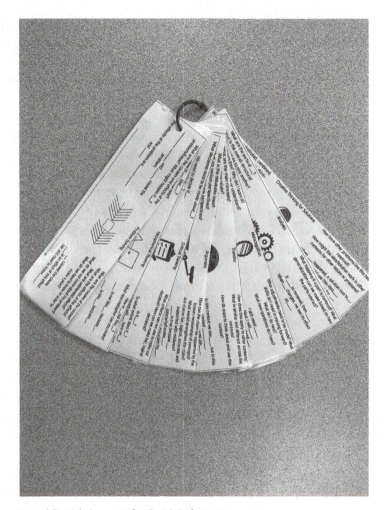

Figure 2.2 Laminated Stretch Prompts for Quick Reference

younger students, twice-exceptional students, or English Language Learners (ELLs). Again, these are not worksheets but scaffolds for supporting students while engaging in discussion using strategic reasoning.

Overall, these Stretch Prompts provide the structure for guiding students towards deeper learning and learning for transfer. In the chapters ahead, you will also see how these Stretch Prompts are linked to specific examples and strategies.

Table 2.4 provides an overview of the strategies in the book and how they align with each Stretch Prompt.

Table 2.4 Stretch Prompts and Related Strategies

Stretch Prompt	Strategy
Analysis	Connections Web Wonder Window See Beyond Schema Board Inductive Reasoning: Group, Re-group, Here's the Scoop POWER Analysis
Problem Solving	Iceberg of Why's Cascade of Consequences Six Thinking Hats
Creative Thinking for Solutions	SCAMPER Stretch Synectic Trigger Mechanisms
Critical Thinking	SWOT Should-Could-Would Criteria
Metaphorical Thinking	Synectic Analogies Forced Associations Extended Synectics Metapatterns
Argument	Argument Construction Model (Elements of Thought) Balloon Debate Argument Techniques
Metacognition	Johari Learning Window Ripple Reflection Mind Maps Reflecting on Relevance WOOP
Transfer	Show You Know Board (Combination of multiple strategies)

3

Strategies for Analysis

[Handwritten annotations: Schema- how we perceive how concepts are connected. 1) exposure 2) engagement 3) elaboration]

A key part of learning involves building upon, structuring, and restructuring schema. Schema is the mental framework that helps us organize and make sense of ideas, experiences, and new knowledge. It is how we perceive how concepts are connected, much like a mental spider web. As we learn new knowledge, this new learning sticks to the structure, and we try to make sense of how it fits with what we already know.

How do we build schema? Schema is built through exposure, engagement, and elaboration. Specifically, students take in new information through visuals, books, videos, or lesson presentations. They make sense of the information by organizing their knowledge and elaborating on its meaning and application to other contexts.

To enhance the development of schema, students must understand how ideas are related to one another. Analysis is all about understanding parts and how they are connected. By understanding these interrelationships, students can uncover the underlying principles and processes that hold the whole together. This synthesis then creates an opportunity for students to make a generalization about the content which can then be applied to real-life situations and other contexts.

The focus of this chapter is on applying the "Analysis" Stretch Prompt (see Figure 3.1). Analysis can simply involve asking students to identify various parts of content (e.g., parts of a plant, sequence of the water cycle, aspects of Roman government, etc.), but students understand the content more deeply when they consider how changing one part affects the overall whole.

[Handwritten annotations: Step 1 then build]

DOI: 10.4324/9781003293286-4

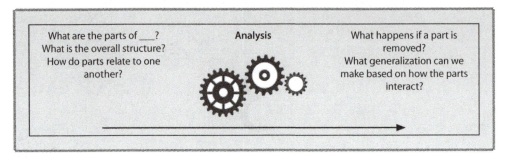

| What are the parts of ___? What is the overall structure? How do parts relate to one another? | Analysis | What happens if a part is removed? What generalization can we make based on how the parts interact? |

Figure 3.1 Analysis Stretch Prompt

Through an emphasis of analysis, students develop an understanding of how the pieces of the content work as a system. Through understanding hierarchies, connections, similarities, differences, and the nature of relationships, students develop more sophisticated schemas for deeper learning.

In some of the strategies that follow, students are given the opportunity to build a foundation for schema, establishing what they already know or asking questions to "get curious" about content they are about to learn (e.g., Wonder Window, See Beyond). These approaches prime students to develop insightful connections when it is time for a deeper analysis. Other strategies allow for students to see relationships between important concepts, perceiving the structure, conceptualizing the relationships, contributions, and connections between ideas, and strengthening their schema; these are all important skills for moving students towards developing expertise.

Strategy #1: Connections Web

Strategy at a Glance

This strategy involves asking students to list the parts, characteristics, or steps of any content on dots around a circle (the strategy works best with 5-20 key terms or concepts). Students discuss connections among the parts or concepts, describing the relationships between the terms. Arrows are drawn on the circle to show the nature of the relationship (sometimes the relationship is cause-effect showing a one-direction arrow; sometimes the relationship is bi-directional, showing arrows in both directions). After connections are made, a web is formed. You can then ask follow-up questions about underlying principles that "hold" the whole together and what would happen if one part was removed. The "stretch" is applied when students develop a generalization about the content—a statement that shows the big idea of the major principle behind the concept connections.

The following are questions to ask while guiding discussion:

1. What cause-effect relationships do you notice?
2. How does ___ contribute to___?
3. What would happen if one part of this was changed? How would it affect the other parts?
4. What causes stability in the web? What causes change?
5. Can you make a sentence with 2–3 words from here that represents a key idea from our learning?
6. How does __ interact with___? What can we learn about each interaction?
7. Which elements seem to be opposites?
8. What do these interactions reveal about balance? What causes imbalance?
9. What big idea statement can we make about how the concepts interact within the entire structure? What can we say is true about the "whole" web?

Source: This model is inspired from analysis wheels created by Stambaugh and Mofield (2022). The Connections Web here can apply to any content area while the analysis wheels are discipline-specific.

Example 1: Motion and Forces

In this example, a teacher teaches a unit about motion and forces. To move towards a deeper understanding of how and why forces affect motion, the teacher might list all the major concepts related to these ideas on the Connections Web, asking students to make connections between concepts.

Here are a few examples of how students can make connections between multiple concepts:

- ◆ Lighter objects (mass) need less force to change speed
- ◆ Forces can stop or change the speed or direction of an object while it is moving
- ◆ Acceleration is change in speed or direction over time
- ◆ Friction is a force that affects inertia
- ◆ Gravity is a force pulling objects together. Gravity is affected by distance between objects and mass.
- ◆ Newton's First Law of Motion explains inertia; if there is zero force, there is zero acceleration
- ◆ Newton's Second Law of Motion explains velocity; the presence of an unbalanced force will accelerate an object

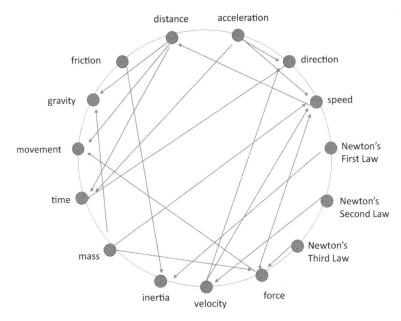

Figure 3.2 Forces and Motions Connections Web

- ◆ Newton's Third Law of Motion explains how force has an equal and opposite reaction
- ◆ Speed is the change in distance over time
- ◆ Velocity is an object's speed in a given direction
- ◆ Speed does not change the mass of an object

Through using some of the sample questions to guide discussion, you might ask, "What do these relationships tell us about change?" Students may conclude that forces change movements of objects, and these changes can be predicted, reflecting the big idea of the unit. Students can then be asked to develop generalizations about the content from these connections. For example:

- ◆ Forces cause objects to move.
- ◆ Interactions between objects and forces allow for prediction

An example of these connections is noted in Figure 3.2.

Example 2: Understanding Geometric Dimensions

The Connections Web can also be applied as students learn mathematical concepts, principles, and formulas. In this example, students can make connections between various aspects of geometric dimensions and ways of measuring perimeter, area, and volume of various one-, two-, and three-dimensional shapes. Using the terms *perimeter, area, faces, rectangles, circles, triangles,* and *volume,* students might create the following connections:

◆ As the perimeter of one side of a face increases, so does area, and so does volume.
◆ Rectangles can be made up of squares and triangles.
◆ If a triangle is rotated, it makes a circle.
◆ A triangle can be inscribed within a circle.
◆ A triangle's area is half of a rectangle's area.
◆ To find the volume of a cube, l, b, and h are all the same.
◆ Volume is like area, except we add the third dimension (rectangle area = bh; cuboid area = lbh; circle area = πr^2).

Through an examination of these connections, students can also understand that when parts are removed (faces of a figure, sides of a shape), other parts are affected.

Through a discussion, the teacher can guide students to arrive at a big idea of the unit such as "shapes can be decomposed into other shapes" or "measurement helps us quantify space and shapes." If working with younger students, the teacher might provide scaffolding by providing a template with a word bank to help students arrive at these generalizations.

These generalizations can be supported with evidence throughout the unit. Students may revisit the Connections Web throughout to demonstrate how new connections between concepts support the generalization.

Other Ideas and Tips

◆ Revisit the Connections Web over the course of a unit for students to continue to make connections to support the generalization or big idea statement.
◆ Use hexagonal thinking as an adaptation of this strategy. Each concept can be written on concept cards in the shapes of hexagons. Students examine the cards and determine the best way to arrange the hexagons to show the relationships between concepts (Potash, 2020). Students should justify why they arranged the concepts as they do and develop a big idea generalization after explaining their connections.
◆ Make this approach interactive by asking students to stand in a circle. Each student would represent a concept, tossing the yarn to another student, articulating the connection between the concepts. Over the course of discussion, a "web" is made from the yarn.
◆ Add complexity to the Connections Web by making an inner circle of separate but somewhat related concepts. Connections can be made

between the concepts of the inner circle alone, then the outer circle alone, and then between the inner and outer circles. For example, the outer circle might include the parts of a plant and how they interact while the inside circle might include concepts related to weather patterns. Overall, this helps students see the big picture of how weather patterns interact with the life cycle of a plant.

Various content applications are provided here.

- ◆ Social Studies:
  - – Key ideas, events, and systems of an ancient society (e.g., Mesopotamia, Egypt, etc.)
  - – Key events of World War I
  - – Fall of the Roman Empire
  - – Causes and Effects of the Great Depression
  - – Implications of the Industrial Revolution
  - – Structure of the Constitution
- ◆ English Language Arts:
  - – Various characters and events of a story; students examine how their interactions influence the unfolding of plot events.
  - – Various points and key ideas within an argument or speech; students examine how these key ideas influence the development of the claim and support the overall argument (See also Stambaugh & Mofield, 2022).
  - – Various parts of speech (e.g., adverbs, predicate nouns, action verbs, adverbs, linking verbs, etc.); students examine how these parts of speech function and influence other parts of speech to convey meaning.
- ◆ Science
  - – Any part of a scientific system (e.g., parts of a cell and their interactions with one another)
  - – Steps within any "process" in science (water cycle, photosynthesis, mitosis, pollination)
  - – Ecosystems and food webs
  - – The interplay between magnetic fields and electrical currents
- ◆ Math
  - – The relationships between fractions, ratios, decimals, and percentages
  - – The relationship between counting by 2, 5, and 10 (and various "multiples")
  - – The relationship between mathematical properties (e.g., association, distributive, identity, etc.) for multiplication and addition

Strategy #2: Wonder Window

Strategy at a Glance

Curiosity is at the heart of life-long learning. This strategy provides opportunities to ignite students' curiosity by prompting students to ask multiple types of questions about a given topic. Students engage in a deep analysis of an image, graph, or text by learning to ask questions with the Wonder Window. Students generate questions in response to a prompt starting with

1. I wonder what. . . ?
2. I wonder why. . . ?
3. I wonder what if. . . ?
4. I wonder how might. . . ?

Difficult for my kids to do

These types of questions encourage thinking from data gathering, analyzing, predicting, and imagining (see Figure 3.3). Throughout any given school day, students respond to question after question, but how often do they have opportunities to pose their own questions in relation to the content? A key part of solving real-world problems (and thinking as an expert) is to know what questions need to be asked. The Wonder Window can encourage exploration of a problem or an issue, setting the stage for next steps in research. The strategy promotes deep engagement, curiosity, and examining evidence, priming the student for for deeper understanding of content. The window also mirrors the "Know, Relate, Extend" structure discussed in Chapter 1.

What? Understand (Know)	What if? Hypothesize (Extend)
Why? Analyze (Relate)	How might? Create/Imagine (Extend)

Figure 3.3 Wonder Window Prompts

	Is, Did, Can	**Would, Will, Might**
Who **What** **When** **Where**	Understand (Know)	Hypothesize (Extend)
How **Why**	Analyze (Relate)	Create/Imagine (Extend)

Figure 3.4 Adapted Q-Matrix

Source: Adapted from Wiederhold and Kagan (1998)

An alternate approach to this method is to use the adapted Q-Matrix (Wiederhold & Kagan, 1998) which prompts students to mix a variety of question words (Who, What, When, Where, How, and Why) with verbs (see Figure 3.4).

This approach allows the student to interact with meaning first, laying the foundation of schema, before students endeavor into deeper learning. This is considered an analysis strategy as it requires students to generate a number of questions from closely examined details and inferences. As students generate their own questions, they are likely to be motivated to pursue and uncover answers later in the lesson or unit.

Teachers may use this strategy with picture book covers, novel covers, graphs displaying data, mathematical formulas, scientific processes (e.g., carbon cycle, food web), the periodic table, a short text or quote, or primary source document. This strategy might set the stage for strategic thinking (DOK Level 3) if students choose to pursue investigating these questions in research, making connections with evidence, and justifying their conclusions. Additionally, the Wonder Window can be used at the end of a unit to inspire future learning. Just as experts continue to ask questions even after a long pursuit of study, we can ignite this type of curiosity in students.

Example 1: Graph Analysis in Science

In this example shown in Figure 3.5, students examine trends of endangered species over time. Depending on the grade level and content, the teacher may use the graph before introducing students to ecosystems or a problem-based learning opportunity where students propose solution ideas to address the issue. This example is applied to "The Number of Endangered Species is Rising: Number of Animal Species of the IUCN Red List, By Class" featuring numbers of mammals, reptiles, birds, insects, amphibians, mollusks, fish, and others from 2007 to the present (see www. statista.com/chart/17122/number-of-threatened-species-red-list/).

• What is the proportion of change in each species? • What is causing this pattern? • What is the role humans play in contributing to these changes?	• What if this trend continues? • What if the mollusks continue to increase exponentially, how will it affect the other species?
• Why are the mollusks increasing more so than the other species? • Why are mammal and bird proportions staying about the same while the other species are changing over time?	• How might we change this trajectory? • How might this affect other systems?

Figure 3.5 Example Responses: Wonder Window—Number of Endangered Species

Example 2: Primary Source Analysis

In this example, students examine various primary source documents related to social reform in the early 20th Century. This might be used as a pre-activity before engaging in a more formal analysis of a primary source document or a study on child labor during this era. You may prompt students to think as a historian, considering questions historians might ask about the primary source. To add another perspective, you may ask students to develop questions by thinking through the point of view of the child.

This activity might be set up as a gallery walk, with various photographs posted throughout the room. As students rotate through the stations, they can add questions to the Wonder Window. Then, students can reflect on patterns they noticed in the photographs.

Figure 3.6 shows possible questions students might ask in response to the Library of Congress source: Hine (1916) "Vera Hill, 5 years old picks 25 pounds a day." www.loc.gov/pictures/item/2018678167/

Other Ideas and Tips

◆ Beyond using the strategy at the beginning or end of a unit to prompt curiosity or further research, you can ask questions before or after a lesson using everyday objects to prompt questions about concepts. For example, a dollar bill or coin might be used to prompt questions to introduce concepts such as symbolism, currency, or economic principles.

◆ Encourage students to ask questions from various perspectives (content areas, stakeholders, etc.).

◆ If used at the introduction of a unit, students can revisit the window as a kind of "KWL" (What do we know? What do we need to know? What have we learned?) activity.

	Is, Did, Can	**Would, Will, Might**
Who **What** **When** **Where**	• When is this (what time of day?) • What is happening in the world during this time?	• What would happen to her if she did not work in the fields? • What would happen if this happened today?
Why **How**	• Why is a 5 year old working? • Why is she not wearing shoes? • Why is she working alone? • How is she feeling? • Why is she not in school?	• How might we know this is authentic and not staged? • Why would parents allow their children to work?

Figure 3.6 Example: Adapted Q-Matrix for Primary Source Document

Source: Q-Matrix is from Wiederhold and Kagan (1998)

- ◆ Complexity can be added by using this strategy with multiple sources as a way for students to answer an essential question.
- ◆ Experts are aware of the questions they ask and the processes used to explore those questions. This strategy encourages metacognition in that it builds an awareness of question-asking as an important skill in collecting data and pursuing learning.

Strategy #3: See Beyond

Strategy at a Glance

"See, Think, Wonder" is a Project Zero thinking routine (Ritchhart et al., 2011) that can be used to ignite curiosity as students examine details and think about an image, primary source, graph, video, book cover, text, or other prompt. Here, it is adapted as "See Beyond" (see Resource 3.1; downloadable at www.routledge.com/9781032275581) to guide students to identify the more abstract concepts and ideas that are represented in the text. Like "See, Think, Wonder," students examine details, make inferences, and ask questions about what they see. To dial this up with more challenge, students then identify the more abstract "concepts" and articulate how these concepts relate to one another. Then, students share how these concepts are seen in other contexts and situations. (This strategy is an adaptation of "See, Think, Wonder" Ritchhart et al., 2011 and "Big Idea Reflection" from Stambaugh & Mofield, 2022).

This is considered an analysis strategy because it allows students to analyze details closely and then to generalize the "idea" represented in the prompt. This allows students to construct meaning by using evidence to

Would work well w/ art and festivals

Details	Thoughts	Questio
What details do you notice? What details are most important?	What are your thoughts about what you see? What might this mean? What do you think happened?	What questior have? What do you want to know? What big question does this raise?

Concepts	Connections	Contexts
What concepts or ideas do you see/notice?	How do the concepts relate to one another? Write a sentence connecting the concepts to reflect the big idea.	How do these ideas relate to the world, you, or other content?

Resource 3.1 See Beyond

Source: Adapted from See, Think, Wonder (Ritchhart et al., 2011) and Big Idea Reflection (Stambaugh & Mofield, 2022)

Art Ex (handwritten)

Details What details do you notice? What details are most important?	Thoughts What are your thoughts about what you see? What might this mean? How do you interpret this?	Questions What questions do you have? What do you want to know? What big question does this raise?
• Ants • Infinity symbol • Never-ending path • One side leads to another side	• It appears the ants are stuck. • Maybe they are unaware they are stuck. • The ants are blindly following each other, with no clear vision on where they are going.	• Are the ants identical? • Who or what is the leader? • What does the structure symbolize? • Why did the artist make this? • Who are what are they following?
Concept What concepts (ideas) do you see?	Connections How do the concepts relate to one another? Write a sentence connecting the concepts to reflect the big idea.	Contexts How do these ideas relate to the world, you, or other content?
status quo routine journey infinity conformity busyness structure cycle powerlessness mindlessness unawareness complacency	When one blindly follows the status quo, one becomes stuck in complacency. We can be unaware of our own conformity. When we are unaware, we do not have the power to change.	This reminds me of how people blindly follow others without questioning the purpose or value of where they are going. This makes me think about my own life where I mindlessly do activities that I think are meaningful, but they do not actually lead to a meaningful goal.

Figure 3.7 Example: See Beyond: Mobius Strip II by M.C. Escher

Source: Example concepts adapted from Stambaugh and Mofield (2018)

uncover big ideas. This strategy is also an opportunity to encourage peer-to-peer dialogue through small group discussions to arrive at conclusions.

Example 1: Art Analysis

In this example, students examine the piece of art, *Mobius Strip II*, by M.C. Escher. This piece of art might be used to introduce ideas related to literature themes (e.g., conformity, leadership, the unexamined life) or related ideas in Social Studies.

Using the See Beyond Strategy (see Figure 3.7), students make observations and generate questions by noting details, thoughts, and questions. Then, students think about the abstract concepts and ideas that are represented in the image. Students are able to pull out big "ideas" when naming concepts they see. From here, students develop a sentence to represent a generalization or main idea statement about the text/art that can also be generalized to real-world contexts. It is important to guide students to identify "ideas" (e.g., conformity, structure, infinity, following) more so than concrete nouns in order to guide students towards generalizing to other contexts.

Additional layers of complexity can be added by asking students to think through a given perspective, compare this art to another piece by the same artist, and research how the historical background of the artist influences the meaning in the work.

Example 2: See Beyond When Reading Text—The Dog and His Bone (Aesop's Fable)

Teachers can use this strategy beyond visual images. Short texts (poems, fables, short stories, chapters in a novel) can also work well if the goal is to guide students to understanding themes and how they translate to real-world contexts. Figure 3.8 shows an example of applying See Beyond to Aesop's fable, *The Dog and His Bone*.

Other Ideas and Tips

- ◆ To dive further into an in-depth analysis of these concepts, you may ask questions about the concepts such as:
  - – How does one concept lead to another concept?
  - – How do events in the story lead to these concepts?
  - – Ask debatable questions about the concepts (e.g., Does the dog experience fear? How?).
  - – Ask questions about the concepts (e.g., What if the dog did not experience _____, how would that affect the rest of the story?).
- ◆ To continue to add complexity to reading the text, students might complete See Beyond for various texts and compare them, specifically by focusing on the bottom row of the table: abstract concepts, how they connect, and how they relate to real-world contexts.

Details	Thoughts	Questions
What details do you notice? What details are most important?	What are your thoughts about what you see? What might this mean? How do you interpret this?	What questions do you have? What do you want to know? What big question does this raise?
• The dog likes bones and is motivated by having a bigger bone. • The dog was distracted. • The dog has regret.	• The dog did not think through his decision. • The dog made the wrong decision. • The dog was fooled by his reflection. • The dog might have been afraid of losing an opportunity to have more.	• How did he think he was going to get the bone from the dog in the river? • Who is his owner? Does he normally get bones? • Is the dog taken care of regularly?
Concepts	Connections	Contexts
What concepts or ideas do you see/notice?	How do the concepts relate to one another? Write a sentence connecting the concepts to reflect the big idea.	How do these ideas relate to the world, you, or other content?
Greed Fear (to lose an opportunity) Contentment Discontentment Regret Ingratitude Security Foolishness	• Greed can lead to loss. • Ingratitude can lead to discontentment. • Wanting more or "fear of missing out" can lead to unwise decisions.	When individuals want "more and more" they often get in debt and lose what they already have.

Figure 3.8 Example: See Beyond—The Dog and His Bone

Strategy #4: Schema Board

Strategy at a Glance

The Schema Board (see Resource 3.2; downloadable at www.routledge.com/9781032275581) provides opportunities for students to elaborate on newly learned concepts, thereby consolidating their conceptual understanding. Students often have issues in learning when there are misconceptions in

Schema Board

Concept_____

Connection to experience	Definition in own words	Sketch of the idea
Example and Non-example	Always Sometimes Never	What is it a part of? What are its parts or categories?
Simile or symbol	What causes ___? What are the effects of ___?	I used to think . . . Now I know . . . Now I will . . .

Resource 3.2 Schema Board

✓ good for "new learning"

their schema or there is a lack of exposure or familiarity with the content. The Schema Board provides a platform for students to thoroughly explore the concept, make connections, and deepen their understanding. Beyond working with the basic understanding of what a concept "is" (first row), students consider classifications, hierarchies, and basic application of the content (second row) to grapple with the structure of the concept. Students then think about the concept more abstractly by connecting it to a simile or symbol, thinking about the implications of the concept, and reflecting on previous misconceptions and new applications of the concept. *3rd Row*

This resource embeds many of the "Science of Learning" strategies (Weinstein et al., 2018) including elaboration, retrieval practice, dual coding, and use of concrete examples. Students elaborate on their learning in multiple ways which develop their use of academic language. Students have opportunities to make meaningful associations from the known (their own lives) to the new. Through this elaboration, dual coding (graphic representation of concepts), and reflecting on their own learning, students develop strong mental structures for organizing new knowledge.

Use Dual Coding in 2 or 3 Step Conjugation

Students could complete the entire board, or you may provide an option for student choice (e.g., choose at least 5 boxes to complete). The Schema Board can be used with the entire class, small groups, pairs of students, or individuals. It can be used throughout a unit as students revisit the concept to deepen their understanding of the content. It is especially useful for "fuzzy" concepts or processes that many students have trouble differentiating (e.g., differences between mood and tone).

Example- Schema Board for Author's Tone

Figure 3.9 shows an example of a completed Schema Board around author's tone in literature.

Other Ideas and Tips

- Individual students, pairs, or small groups might be assigned various terms used throughout a unit of study. For example, terms related to a unit on laws of motion (1st, 2nd, 3rd law, acceleration, gravity, etc.) can be assigned and reviewed in a jigsaw fashion.
- Students can choose to complete the board as a tic-tac-toe vertical column or diagonal (to ensure they include foundational, conceptual, and abstract thinking).
- Students may revisit the Schema Board throughout a unit to add new connections and ideas.
- Students may bring in concrete objects to represent their symbols or similes.

Basic understanding	**Connection to experience** Tone reminds me of my mother saying "don't use that tone of voice with me."	**Definition in own words** The way authors sound in their writing. It shows their point of view towards the idea in the text.	**Sketch of the idea** Person speaking into a microphone— shows the "voice" of the author
Conceptual understanding	**Example and non-example** Example- The tone in "Stopping by the Woods on a Snowy Evening" is contemplative. Non-example: Mood of a story is how a reader feels.	**Always Sometimes Never** Tone always conveys the author's intention. Tone is sometimes created from dialogue. Tone is never outright stated in text as "this is the tone." Tone has to be inferred.	**What is it a part of? What are its parts or categories?** Tone is a literary element that helps shape the meaning and interpretation of a story. Tone can be positive, neutral, or negative with various nuances.
Abstract understanding/ Metacognition	**Simile or Symbol** Tone is like a special microphone with special effects that can be adjusted. The author "speaks" the message with words, making intentional adjustments (sound effects) to emphasize attitude toward the content in the text.	**What causes__? What are the effects of__?** Other literary elements affect the development of the tone. The tone influences the reader's interpretation of the text.	**I used to think__ Now I know__ Now I will___** I used to think tone was mainly about feelings I feel when I read. Now I know it is about the author's voice and attitude. Now I will intentionally use specific words to change tone.

Figure 3.9 Example of Schema Board for Author's Tone

- Often, the most difficult part for students is in understanding what the concept is a part of and what are its parts. Students may expand on this by creating hierarchical concept maps to solidify their understanding.
- Guide students towards DOK Level 3 strategic thinking by continuing to ask students how parts of the concept interact and how a change in one part affects the other parts (e.g., imagery and figurative language can affect tone).
- Use the Schema Board as a foundation for learning a concept so that students can apply the concept to more complex reasoning tasks (e.g., creative problem solving, critical thinking, etc.). For example, after working through the Schema Board with "tone," students might revise a given poem, changing its tone by modifying other literary elements.

Strategy #5: Inductive Reasoning—"Group, Re-Group, Here's the Scoop"

Strategy at a Glance

Concept development is well known in gifted education curriculum. Often referred to as The Concept Development Model (Taba et al., 1971), it is an inductive reasoning approach for students to classify key ideas and make generalizations about the concept being studied.

First, students sort various terms, ideas, people, etc. from a unit of study. You can provide students a list of the terms on a sheet of paper; however, this strategy is more engaging if the words are cut out so they can be easily sorted and re-sorted by students. Students must analyze patterns to determine how terms are alike or different from one another. They label these categories, applying strategic reasoning by justifying why they grouped content in this way. Students are then asked to "re-sort" the terms again, considering alternative ways to see patterns in the terms. From here, students synthesize their learning and develop summary statements or generalizations about the content ("here's the scoop"—the big takeaway or big idea).

This strategy can be used at the beginning of a unit to understand what students might already know about content, serving as a pre-assessment. Before content is introduced, students sort the terms into groups, then re-sort the words, and write down a "big idea statement" or prediction regarding the content. Throughout the unit, students can revisit the statement to determine if their big idea statement is supported or not. If the content is too unfamiliar,

Table 3.1 Tiered Tasks for Inductive Reasoning: Group-Regroup—Here's the Scoop

Tier 1	Tier 2	Tier 3
1. Provide words and categories. 2. Students place words into categories. 3. Students are given new categories to regroup. 4. Students develop hypotheses and/or generalizations.	1. Provide words (without categories). 2. Students develop their own categories to sort the words. 3. Students are asked to regroup their words into new categories. 4. Students develop hypotheses and/or generalizations.	1. Ask students to list ideas/words they know about the topic. 2. Students develop their own categories to sort the words. 3. Students are asked to regroup into other categories. 4. Students develop hypotheses and/or generalizations.

then it might be best to use this strategy mid-way through a unit. In this way, students apply reasoning to justify the categories and can make more sophisticated generalizations about the content.

This task can be easily tiered for students with varying levels of complexity (see Table 3.1). For example, for students who might need support in their learning, the task can be differentiated by providing the category labels to students. For students who already know some of the content, the task can be made more open-ended by requiring students to generate a list of words associated with the content.

Example 1: Geological Features

At the beginning of a unit on Earth's geological features, the teacher provides a list of landforms and other words related to a unit in Earth Science. The teacher uses this activity to expose students to new academic language by providing access to various resources and materials. In this case, as students work with unfamiliar terms, they look up terms and make decisions about the relationships between the concepts.

- ◆ Step 1: Group—Provide students with a list of terms (see Figure 3.10). Ask students to sort these terms into categories and to label their categories. Encourage students to focus their categories as they relate to "Science" (otherwise students might sort alphabetically or by nouns and verbs, which does not help them arrive at a meaty summary statement or generalization).

mountain	sediment	delta	physical weathering
plateau	erosion	rock sculptures	chemical weathering
plain	deposition	glaciers	sand dunes
soil	wind	deformation	river
valley	canyon	volcanoes	

Figure 3.10 Word List Used for Concept Development Model

◆ Step 2: Justify—Ask students to justify their categories. Why did they sort them as they did? What 's similar about the terms within a group?
◆ In the first sort, students might develop the following categories:
    – **Processes that Cause Change**—erosion, deposition, physical weathering
    – **Things that Move that Cause Change**—soil, sediment, wind, river
    – **Landforms**—mountains, plains, plateaus, valley, canyon, delta, rock sculptures, glaciers, volcanos, sand dune
◆ Step 3: Re-group—Ask students to re-sort the terms into new categories. This is often a challenge and requires a close examination of the relationships between the concepts. Again, students should justify why they sorted as they did:
    – **Related to Movement of Water**—soil, sediment, deposition, canyon, delta, river, erosion
    – **Related to Tectonic Plates**—plateau, valley, volcanoes
    – **Related to Climate**—wind, rock sculptures, glaciers, sand dunes, physical weathering, chemical weathering
◆ Step 4: Here's the Scoop—Guide students to develop "big idea" statements that connect all of their categories. For fun with students, you could say, "What's the scoop? What's a true statement about all of these categories?" You might ask the following questions to provide scaffolding:
    – What patterns did you notice?
    – What cause-effect relationships did you notice?
    – What is the big idea of geological features?
    – What do you think might be a "true statement" we can make about geological features? We can check to see if this statement holds true throughout our study.
    – How are these categories related to each other?

◆ As students discuss responses, they might arrive at the following generalizations:
  – Various processes shape the land.
  – The Earth keeps changing.
  – Water and wind shape the earth.
  – The Earth changes because of what's under the ground and above the ground.

◆ Step 5: Support—Post these generalizations in the classroom, and throughout the unit, revisit them, asking students to provide evidence supporting them. If some of the generalizations are not always "true statements," then ask students how they might be revised throughout the unit.

Other Ideas and Tips

◆ Challenge students by not allowing them to create an "other" category.

◆ Challenge students by asking them to create mini categories from their larger categories or asking what other terms (not on the list) might be added to these categories.

◆ Encourage students to think about how terms might belong in more than one category.

◆ This activity can also be used at the end of a unit as more of a summative assessment approach. As students develop generalizations, they can support those generalizations with other facts and details learned throughout the unit (beyond the terms provided).

◆ This strategy can also work well as a bookend (both at the beginning and end of a lesson) when reading text. For example, before students read a nonfiction text about the Industrial Revolution, you may choose key terms for students to sort and make a hypothesis about the main idea of the text. This builds schema for students to link new information to as they read a text. Then, after the text is read, they can re-sort the terms and revise their generalizations.

◆ As students create generalizations about the content and determine evidence that supports or refutes it, you might ask follow-up questions:
  – Are these generalizations *always* true?
  – In what situations are they only *sometimes* true?
  – Are there other content areas where we see this big idea (e.g., can the generalizations about Ancient Greece be said of other civilizations as well)?

Strategy #6: POWER Analysis

Strategy at a Glance

The acronym of POWER can be used to guide students to critically examine the role of power in literature, nonfiction, visual art, primary sources, and other media. This tool provides prompts for thinking about issues related to social justice, politics, and messages in media sources. Resource 3.3 (downloadable at www.routledge.com/9781032275581) can be used by students to record responses. Through a POWER analysis, students can think about how the parts come together to reveal a source of influence. The prompts are as follows:

- ◆ P—Who has the power in this source? What is the source of the power? What is the type of power? What is concealed and revealed through power?
- ◆ O—What is left out of this source/story?
- ◆ W—Why was this source made?
- ◆ E—How does this source evoke emotion and/or empathy?
- ◆ R—What is your response to this text/source?

Example—Primary Source Document for Women's Suffrage

In this example, students study the primary source document "The Sky in Now Her Limit" by Elmer Andrews Bushnell (August 1920). Through applying the POWER Analysis, students gain deeper insight into the message of the document. Sample responses might include the following:

- ◆ P—The young, burdened woman has access to the highest source of power (Presidency), though it is a long road ahead. The source of being able to attain the highest source of power is connected to the middle rung of equal suffrage. The type of power to be attained is the ultimate power of influence in government office. This source reveals the contrast between the lower rungs and highest rungs. The highest rungs are most difficult to see (somewhat concealed). The image reveals a path, but it does not illuminate the barriers of reality along the way.
- ◆ O—Other ethnicities are not represented.
- ◆ W—The author's purpose might be to show that women suffrage is one more step towards gaining access to the highest forms of power.
- ◆ E—This evokes a sense of cautious optimism. There is hope in women obtaining more power, but we can also sense the burden the young girl might feel in progressing up the ladder.

POWER Analysis

Analyze the text by reflecting on each component of POWER.

Analysis Questions	Response
P—Who has the power in this source? What is the source of the power? What is the type of power? What is concealed and revealed through power?	
O—What is left <u>out</u> of this source/story?	
W—Why was this source made?	
E—How does this evoke <u>emotions</u> and/or empathy?	
R—What is your <u>response</u> to this text/source?	

Resource 3.3 POWER Analysis

- ◆ R—This makes me think of my own great grandmothers who climbed the ladder. Through each generation, women progressed higher and higher on the ladder.

Example 2: POWER Analysis applied to Icarus and Daedalus

Students read the Greek myth "Icarus and Daedalus" and reflect on its message as it relates to the limits of power.

- ◆ P—Icarus gained power (the ability to escape Crete) by using waxed wings. This source of power was Daedalus' creation, but in the end, this creation was not more powerful than nature (the Sun). This revealed that there are limits to human invention and freedom. Icarus's ambition concealed his perspective of reality as he was wrapped up in his pursuit of flying higher.
- ◆ O—This story leaves out an opportunity for Icarus to learn from his mistake (since the story ends with his death).

- ◆ W—This story might have been written to provide a lesson about understanding one's limits or how pleasure can cloud one's judgment.
- ◆ E—This story evokes a sense of regret for Icarus
- ◆ R—We often believe that freedom and success are a result of having power, but there are unexpected consequences from having too much freedom or success.

Other Ideas and Tips

- ◆ Students can apply the POWER Analysis to short movie clips, popular songs, commercials, and other ads to critically analyze messages.

This tool works well as a reflection prompt after the use of See Beyond Strategy or the Wonder Window.

4

Strategies for Problem Solving

Understanding the Problem

In education, we ultimately want students to apply learning in order to solve real-world issues and problems. When experts solve problems within their fields, they do not do so haphazardly; rather, they pinpoint the nature of the problem, analyze its root cause, and think through outcomes of multiple solution ideas. Such an approach can also be taught to students. To best facilitate students to "be creative" and propose solution ideas for various problems (see Chapter 5), we can provide structures for students to think through a problem, guiding them to understand the underlying cause-effect relationships and forecast short and long-term consequences of solution ideas.

The strategies in this chapter focus on the "Problem Solving" Stretch Prompt (see Figure 4.1).

Each strategy can be used to guide students to dive deeper into the "why" behind various problems or issues. These approaches work especially well as

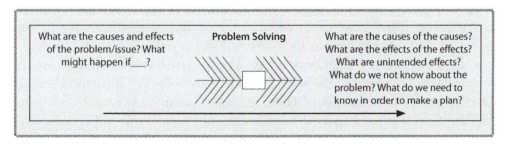

Figure 4.1 Problem Solving Stretch Prompt

DOI: 10.4324/9781003293286-5

part of problem-based learning (PBL) units, though they can be embedded into any lesson to encourage students to understand complex cause-effect relationships or proposing a plan for new and improved ideas. Therefore, these are excellent examples as prompts for DOK Level 3 tasks as students analyze complex interrelationships, make decisions considering future consequences, and modify ideas to improve solutions. Some of these strategies focus on problem identification while others focus on developing solution ideas. They work hand in hand because in order to really solve a problem, you must first understand it and uncover what needs to be known before moving forward.

Strategy #7: Iceberg of Why's

Strategy at a Glance

This strategy is used to help students understand what's below the surface of a given problem. What we often see as a problem is "surface level," but we cannot really address the problem until we understand why the problem exists. Much like Toyoda's 5 Why strategy developed by the Japanese inventor in the 1930's (MindTools, n.d.), this strategy prompts students to continue to ask a series of "why" questions to determine what's below the surface of a problem. Students examine layers of the issue using the following structure:

Why___?
because____
because ____
because ____
so___

Understanding the root of the problem can set the stage for developing solutions that actually address the problem.

As I write this, I'm looking out my window noticing moles have wreaked havoc on our yard. I can easily identify the problem—moles are tearing up our yard. But what exactly is the nature of this problem? Why are moles in our yard but not our neighbors' yard? The answer? There is a food source in our yard. To get rid of the moles, we need to get rid of their food source. But is there more to consider? There are holes in our yard *because* moles are seeking food. They are seeking food in our yard *because* our soil is damp and attracts earthworms. Our soil is damp and attracts earthworms *because* water

from our neighbors' yard drains into our yard. *So*, the extra water cou
the main problem. This leads me to the question "Should we are structure the
drainage system?"

This strategy works by asking follow-up why questions to a Key Question with a structure such as the following (you may write the questions on
the board to show the structure of an iceberg):

- Why? (Key Why Question):
  - Because . . .
- Follow-Up Why Question:
  - Because . . .
- Follow-Up Why Question:
  - Because . . .
- So . . .
  - Conclusion—should answer Key Question at a deeper level,
    prompt next steps, or lead to a new big question

[handwritten note: might be good for Cornerstones ↓]

Example 1: Overpopulation of Deer

In Science, students explore real-world issues related to their community in a
unit on ecosystems. Students share that they have family members involved
in car wrecks because deer run in front of their cars. Students propose the
question, "Why are there so many deer in our community?" The Iceberg of
Why's can help students arrive at conclusions. Here is an example of how a
teacher might facilitate this activity:

- Key Why Question: Why is there an overpopulation of deer in our
  community?
  - *Because* there is a lack of predators in their natural habitat.
    (Teacher can connect this to what students know about balancing
    ecosystems).
- Follow-Up Why Question: Why is there a lack of predators?
  - *Because* natural environments have become smaller and smaller.
- Follow-Up Why Question: Why is their environment becoming
  smaller and smaller?
  - *Because* the building of roads, homes, and other new construction
    has interfered with their environment.
- Conclusion: What conclusion can we make from our answers to our
  Key Why Question?
  - *So*, human progress is interfering with natural systems. This
    connects to the big idea of interdependence.

Example 2: Analyzing a Problem in *The Giver*

This strategy also works well when examining any problem or issue in a text, story, or poem.

- ◆ Key Why Question: Why are the characters in *The Giver* content in dystopian society?
  - – *Because* there is little conflict within their world.
- ◆ Follow-Up Why Question: Why is there little conflict?
  - – *Because* society emphasizes sameness and suppression of emotion.
- ◆ Follow-Up Why Question: Why does their society emphasize sameness and suppression of emotion?
  - – *Because* the society seeks to control its citizens.
- ◆ What conclusion can we make to answer the Key Why Question? What big questions does this raise?
  - – *So*, we see an interesting paradox—They are content because they are unaware of how they are controlled. In order to not be controlled, they must realize they are controlled, but would they still be content?

Example 3: Understanding Character Motives

This strategy can also help students understand the underlying motives of characters and their actions. As readers they observe the behaviors of the characters, but through making inferences, they can uncover underlying motives (the why) behind their actions. This can often help students understand the big idea or lesson of a story. The following is an example applied to "The Three Little Pigs."

- ◆ Key Question: Why is the brother pig looking for a place to live?
  - – *Because* he is too lazy to build one himself.
- ◆ Follow-up Question: Why is he too lazy to build one himself?
  - – *Because* he wants to spend time doing other things.
- ◆ Follow-up Question: Why does he want to spend time doing other things?
  - – *Because* this is more appealing to his interests, and he does not see the long-term repercussions of his actions.
- ◆ What conclusion can we make to answer the Key Why Question? What big questions does this raise?
  - – *So*, the pig is most interested in the present moment and has not thought of the long-term effects of his actions. Is it right for this pig to seek refuge with his brother in the brick house?

Little kids "Why" questions (they question everything)

Other Tips and Ideas

◆ The strategy can work with multiple "because statements." It is not necessary to include only three "because statements" in the structure.

◆ Use this strategy to connect content to real-world issues. For example, in studying the current issue of increased obesity rates, students can understand the cultural, economic, and social causes of the issue (e.g., busy lifestyles and cost of healthy food).

◆ This strategy can enhance discussions related to nonfiction texts. As students determine the problem within the text, they can make inferences as to why the problem occurred.

◆ This can be useful in understanding the underlying issues of historical events and movements.

◆ Students may revisit their Iceberg of Why's throughout a unit to support their initial answers with more evidence as they progress in their learning. Using the "Problem Solving" Stretch Prompt will also encourage students to think through what they still need to know about the problem.

◆ While seemingly simple, this strategy can often lead to students arriving at thought-provoking conclusions. Guide students to identify paradoxes in their conclusions (as in *The Giver* example) or surprising connections.

◆ Complexity can be added to this strategy by creating multiple paths for multiple answers to the key question. If more than one answer is offered for the Key Question, then you might ask follow-up questions to each new path.

Strategy #8: Cascade of Consequences

Strategy at a Glance

The purpose of this strategy is to guide students in understanding second-order effects, that is, every action has a consequence, and every consequence has a subsequent consequence. Beyond the simple cause-effect analysis, students consider a series of consequences from problems and issues, including short-term, long-term, positive, negative, intended, and unintended consequences.

This strategy can be used in a number of ways:

1. Consider long-term effects of a problem or issue.
2. Consider long-term effects of a decision, event, or contribution in history.

3. Consider long-term effects of proposed decisions. Students can think through "what if" scenarios, following how consequences lead to subsequent consequences.

To provide the "stretch," it is also important to ask students to think through unintended consequences to an issue.

This skill is important because it translates to developing decision-making skills, especially applied to real-world problem solving. For example, a seemingly positive solution to a problem might lead to unforeseen negative consequences. The smartphone is an excellent example. This innovative piece of technology is a convenient way for humans to communicate, but it has also led to distracted driving, which has led to car accidents. As we prepare students to be creative problem solvers, the skill of thinking through second-order effects can help them see the complexities of how actions can lead to broad implications.

To introduce this concept to students, you can share the Cobra effect phenomenon. The Cobra effect is when a solution to the problem makes the problem worse. In the early 20th century, there was a huge rat population in Hanoi causing major health concerns. To address the problem, people were encouraged to kill rats. They were rewarded for doing so if they showed proof of killing the rats by presenting rat tails. As a result, tailless rats were sighted throughout the city! What happened? People had started illegally breeding rats for their tails in order to make money!

Example 1: Overuse of Plastics

In this example, students examine multiple effects of an environmental problem. Plastics were invented as a seemingly positive solution to manufacture goods because they are not dependent entirely on natural resources in the environment. However, plastics do not biodegrade. The EPA reports "every bit of plastic ever made still exists." Students can research the lasting repercussions of plastics on marine life, the ocean, rivers, soils, and groundwater. As students work in small groups, they develop their own Cascade of Consequences map to show how effects lead to other effects (see Figure 4.2 as an example). Note that there can be more than one effect from an effect; students can create multiple branches and paths to show cause-effect relationships. Through establishing how effects lead to effects, students can see the severity of a problem, especially if it continues long term.

Example 2: The Effects of the Industrial Revolution

This strategy can also be used to study broad implications of historical events or movements. This can be completed as students progress through a unit

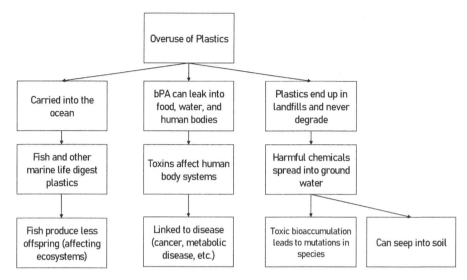

Figure 4.2 Cascade of Consequences: Effects of Overuse of Plastics

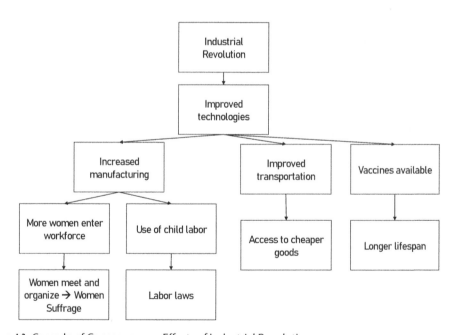

Figure 4.3 Cascade of Consequences: Effects of Industrial Revolution

or used at the end of a unit as a summative assessment. In this example, the model guides students to understand the interrelationships between technology, culture, and political movements. Figure 4.3 shows an example of applying the strategy to the Industrial Revolution.

Other Ideas and Tips

- ◆ After students identify a number of consequences, they can label consequences that relate to various categories or even positive or negative implications. This works especially well when students think through possible "solutions" such as laws. For example, "What if___ was made a law? What would the consequences be?"
- ◆ This model can also work well in thinking through "What if" scenarios in history such as "What might have happened if the 19th Amendment for women's right to vote was originally part of the Constitution?" Thinking through the what-if scenario prompts students to imagine how changes in history would have large repercussions on the present.
- ◆ Students can think through alternative endings to stories in literature. For example, "What if a character had made a different decision? How might the story play out differently?" Students can map out multiple scenarios and plot sequences.
- ◆ Students can use the model as a decision-making strategy. For example, the top box might indicate a debatable question, "Should grocery stores stop the use of plastic bags?" where students think through the long-term implications of both yes and no perspectives.
- ◆ Students can apply the model to making a decision related to their own lives (e.g., consequences of getting a new pet, playing on a sports team, etc.)
- ◆ The Double Fishbone model as shown in Figure 4.4 is a similar tool that can be used to guide students to understand multiple

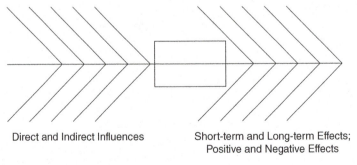

Direct and Indirect Influences   Short-term and Long-term Effects;
                                        Positive and Negative Effects

Figure 4.4 Double Fishbone Model

Source: Republished with permission of Taylor and Francis, from Collaboration, Coteaching, and Coaching in Gifted Education: Sharing Strategies to Support Gifted Learners, Mofield, E., & Phelps, V. (2020), permission conveyed through Copyright Clearance Center, Inc.

effects (antecedents) of the event/issue as well as the consequences. An issue, problem, or event is placed in the center. Students note both causes and effects of the issue on the diagram. For example, students might consider all the indirect and direct causes of the Industrial Revolution (e.g., agricultural revolution; government policies encouraging growth) as well as the effects. This can provide a foundation for thinking before students use the Cascade of Consequences model to visualize even more "effects of the effects" through multiple paths.

not just "my idea is THE right idea"

Strategy #9: Six Thinking Hats

Strategy at a Glance

The Six Thinking Hats (de Bono, 1985/2016) is a tool for analyzing a problem or issue from multiple perspectives. This is relevant to the focus of this chapter because it allows students to see an issue or solution idea from various angles. Additionally, it helps students identify and define the nature of a problem. In the context of dimensions of creativity, this strategy enhances flexible thinking, which is the ability to develop *varied* ideas.

The basic model includes thinking through the following perspectives:

◆ Yellow hat—identifies benefits and positive attributes
◆ Black hat—exercises caution, critical judgment, and evaluation
◆ Red hat—uses intuition, emotion, gut instinct, feelings (without the need to justify)
◆ Green hat—generates new ideas and possibilities
◆ White hat—identifies facts, information, and what needs to be known
◆ Blue hat—aims for the big picture, considers priorities, summarizes, concludes; reflects on process.

This strategy is not new in gifted education. It indeed presents an opportunity for students to see various perspectives; yet, students can do more with this model than simply think through each hat. When this strategy is integrated with Paul's Elements of Thought (see Chapter 2), more complexity is added in considering the various perspectives. Resource 4.1 (downloadable at www.routledge.com/9781032275581) is a template that can be used to facilitate thinking with additional layers of reasoning within the Six Thinking Hats.

Issue
(Problem, Solution Idea, Debatable Question)

Red Hat
- What is my initial reaction?
- What are my gut feelings?
- What are my underlying *assumptions*?
- What would these emotions lead to? (*implications*)

White Hat
- What do we know?
- Is the *evidence* valid?
- What do we still need to know?
- Are we making valid *inferences*?

Yellow Hat
- What are the benefits?
- What positive aspects do I see?
- What are the underlying *assumptions* of these benefits?
- What are the effects of these benefits? (*implications*)

Green Hat
- What else might we do?
- What are the possibilities of this?
- What if ___?
- What does this allow? What else?
- What are the *assumptions* in these possibilities?
- What are the positive and negative effects of these new possibilities? (*implications*)

Blue Hat
- What is the major *purpose* of ___?
- What is the big idea? What is the underlying issue? (*concept*)
- What criteria should we use to make our decision? (*evidence*)
- What are our big ideas or conclusions?
- What are the long-term effects/*implications* to consider?
- How are we approaching our thinking?
- How should we adjust our thinking?

Black Hat
- What might go wrong?
- What are the obstacles?
- What are the underlying *assumptions* in these cautions?
- What are the effects of this criticism? (*implications*)

Source: Adapted from de Bono (1985/2016) and Paul and Elder (2019)

Student Handout

Directions: Use the Six Hats Thinking Model to think about the issue from many perspectives.

Issue		
Red Hat Emotions/Gut Reaction	**White Hat** Facts/Evidence	**Yellow Hat** Benefits
Green Hat Possibilities	**Blue Hat** Reflection on Thinking	**Black Hat** Caution

Resource 4.1 Six Thinking Hats with Elements of Reasoning

Source: Adapted from de Bono (1985/2016) and Paul and Elder (2019)

Cadet
Conversions

Issue

Should we build a mega-market in our community?

White Hat	Yellow Hat
• We know that planners are looking to build a mega-market in the heart of town. • We will need to know when this will happen. • We need to know what store it will be.	• Citizens will not have to drive to the other side of town to go shopping. • Tax money will go towards the city. • Assumption: people prefer convenience and financial benefits • People will save time (+) because they shop nearby • New construction hurts ecosystems. (implications)

Blue Hat	Black Hat
• Importance: addresses needs of citizens • Main idea: access to goods and services (Concepts: access, goods, community) • Criteria: Does it bring new opportunities? • Does it hurt other businesses? • Would citizens shop here? etc. • Long-term implications: More opportunities for city growth and development	• Might compete with local "mom and pop" shops in the community. • Might cause traffic issues. The growth makes the small town not so "small." • Assumption: Citizens would not want local businesses to be negatively affected. • Planners might consider the perspectives of local businesses (+) and continue to support them. • Too much criticism might lead to a complete rejection of the city's growth.

Red Hat	Green Hat
• Emotion: fear, disappointment, gut reaction could be negative • Assumption: Small businesses may be negatively affected. City is growing too quickly. • Implication: these emotions might lead to people voicing their opinions to the city planners, etc. Residents could move to smaller communities. *Depending on stakeholder—emotions could be excitement, eagerness, relief etc.*	• This might bring in new job opportunities. • Other smaller businesses may lease nearby (e.g., hair salons, office buildings) • Assumption: businesses will want to be near the mega-market • More opportunities for others (+) • This could bring more traffic to the area (–) (implications)

Figure 4.5 Example: Six Thinking Hats with Elements of Paul's Reasoning—Building A Mega-Market

In the example shown in Figure 4.5, students reason through the issue of "Should we build a mega-market within our community?" while engaged in a Social Studies lesson about goods, services, consumers, and producers. Beyond thinking through the emotions, benefits, cautions, facts, conclusions, and new ideas, students dig deeper into the assumptions and implications of many of these perspectives while also intentionally considering the purpose, concepts, and major inferences of their reasoning.

Example 2: Text Analysis

The Six Thinking Hats can be used as a way for students to generate questions about decisions characters make throughout a story. Rather than students responding to teacher-provided questions, students might respond to the various Six Thinking Hat prompts from character perspectives. Using "Icarus and Daedalus" as an example, from the perspective of Icarus, students might examine Icarus's decision through the Six Thinking Hats. What were his emotions? What benefits did he perceive? What other options did he have? What facts did he rely on?

You can also prepare prompts for Socratic Seminars on short texts, poems, fables, and primary source documents using the Six Thinking Hat prompts. For example, students might think through all the hats as they apply to advice provided in Rudyard Kipling's "If." Which statements would bring the most benefit (yellow) to you personally right now? Which statements would you be most cautious of (black)? How do your emotional reactions differ on these (red)? What possibilities do these statements evoke (green)? What decisions need to be made when applying this advice (white)? etc.

This strategy can be especially relevant when students read any nonfiction text (from Newsela, Scholastic, etc.) or research an issue in depth. For example, students might extend their thinking by understanding and defining problems around the following topics:

◆ What if the minimum wage increased by 10%? 〕 for Math
◆ What are all the effects of commuter traffic?
◆ Should we build a new playground?

The strategy is useful in a variety of content areas. For example, in Social Studies, students can consider various perspectives on historical events (e.g., transcontinental railroad, The Monroe Doctrine, The New Deal, etc.) and primary source documents.

Other Ideas and Tips

◆ Avoid locking stakeholders into "hats." For example, students can consider how an individual or stakeholder thinks through all the hats. A stakeholder can have both positive (yellow) and cautious (black) perspectives on an idea while also having emotions (red) and seeing many possibilities (green). In the example above about building a mega-market in a community, a small business owner, new community member, and a realtor perspective can have multi-faceted views of the issue.

◆ Guide students to think about how the various hats connect with one another. For example, various possibilities (green) can lead to positive (yellow) and negative (black) outcomes. As new data is presented (white), this can lead to initial emotions (red). Outlining the criteria needed to make a decision (blue) can lead to the need to develop new possibilities (green).

◆ Be creative with Six Thinking Hats! Students can make their own hats, wear colored neckties, or simply represent the hat color with a marker in a chalk talk as they discuss the issue.

Because the purpose of Six Thinking Hats is to uncover new insight related to a problem or issue, it is important to plan time for students to reflect on any new patterns or ideas that emerge from this experience.

5

Strategies for Problem Solving

Creating and Evaluating Solutions

The strategies in this chapter provide structures for supporting students in thinking of and evaluating creative solution ideas. Often when students are engaged in project or problem-based learning, they are often required to develop creative solutions; yet, they need a structure to guide their thinking beyond a random brainstorming of ideas. In the context of Depth of Knowledge, the strategies in this chapter bring students to engage in DOK Level 3 where students judge and evaluate ideas (e.g., SWOT, Should-Could-Would Criteria), and DOK Level 4 where students improve, create, and transfer solutions to new contexts (e.g., SCAMPER, Synectic Trigger Mechanisms). Further, these strategies support many of the objectives in the Taxonomy of Creative Thinking (see Chapter 2), especially as they relate to making connections across ideas (e.g., students will combine part of existing ideas to generate original extensions of those ideas). They also support several of the objectives in the combined Creativity and Critical Thinking Matrix such as evaluating proposed ideas for credibility, relevance, and significance. This chapter focuses on the Stretch Prompts "Creative Thinking for Solutions" and "Critical Thinking" as shown in Figure 5.1.

Strategy #10: The SCAMPER Stretch

Strategy at a Glance
SCAMPER (Eberle, 2008) is a thinking tool for lateral thinking and a creative thinking approach for seeing a problem or solution in a new way. Using this

DOI: 10.4324/9781003293286-6

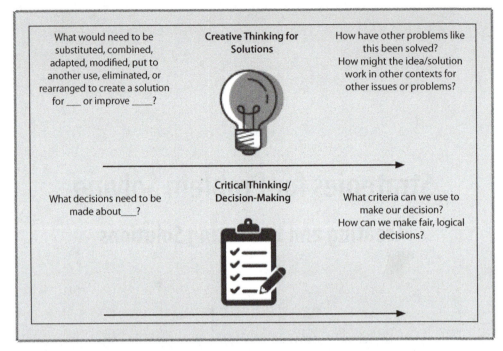

Figure 5.1 Creative Thinking for Solutions and Critical Thinking Stretch Prompts

acronym, students can think about how all ideas are adaptations of previous ideas. Like Six Thinking Hats, it is useful for developing skills in creative thinking, especially fluency (thinking of many ideas) and flexibility (thinking of varied ideas). SCAMPER provides seven question prompts for considering how a current idea can be changed or modified in some way to improve it. Using SCAMPER is an excellent way for students to explore "What if" questions and think strategically when adapting or improving ideas. The prompts are as follows:

- ◆ S—Substitute
- ◆ C—Combine
- ◆ A—Adapt
- ◆ M—Modify (Minimize or Maximize)
- ◆ P—Put to Other Use
- ◆ E—Eliminate
- ◆ R—Reverse

SCAMPER can be used after students have applied other previously mentioned strategies to understand and define a problem. For example, while thinking about the causes of harmful chemicals in plastic wastes which lead to polluted air, soil, and water, students can apply SCAMPER to develop ideas for reducing the use of plastics in everyday life. The prompts can inspire ideas that may not yet be realistic but could be in the future with break-through technologies.

- How might we *substitute* the plastic products with non-plastic products (e.g., Ziplock bags, grocery bags, water bottles)? What would the long-term effect be if a family of four committed to this for one year?
- What if we *combine* the efforts of school cafeterias to also commit to using less plastic? What would be the effect if our school district committed to this for one year?
- What if plastic could be immediately recycled (*adapted*) in new ways in our own home (e.g., grocery bags, old toys, etc. could be melted and re-made into a product of our choice)?
- What if we *modify* how storm drains are used, with more careful tracking of the water before it leads to streams, rivers, and eventually the ocean?
- What needs to be *eliminated* from plastics to make them more easily recycled and repurposed?
- What if we *reversed* the "convenience" of plastics? Might we consider a penalty or special tax placed on plastic goods? If plastics are made from petroleum, might we *reverse* the process so that plastic can be re-made into petroleum for fuel?

The Stretch

SCAMPER is excellent to use when brainstorming solutions to a given problem. In the context of extended thinking in the Depth of Knowledge framework, SCAMPER can be used to apply ideas from previous situations and transfer ideas to other contexts (as shown in the Stretch Prompt, Figure 5.1).

For example, as students brainstorm ideas, students might consider how similar problems were solved in other contexts. If thinking through reducing plastic waste, students might ask "How have we reduced the use of paper in the past 20 years?" Through the use of technology, many newspapers and books are now in electronic form. Many individuals have switched from reading newspapers on paper to reading it on their phones because of convenience. A discussion such as this might lead to new ideas for reducing plastics: "How might we *modify* (apply each element of SCAMPER) our lives so that it is more convenient *not* to use plastics?"

The stretch can also be applied after students engage in Problem Solving. For example, you may ask, "Can we think of other contexts in which these new solutions might apply?" Perhaps students can apply similar ideas to reducing water use or more efficiently recycling other materials.

Example 1: SCAMPER + Attributes with Literary Elements

This example shows how SCAMPER can be used in conjunction with "attribute" listing in which students list the features or attributes of a given object or idea (much like the "parts" on a Connections Web in Chapter 3). The following example shows literary elements of a story listed with SCAMPER. Using the structure of a grid as in Figure 5.2, students can brainstorm possibilities for aspects of the story to change. After brainstorming ideas, students might select one or two aspects to create a new version of the story. To provide an additional stretch, students might think about how changing these same elements in other stories might produce similar patterns in a story's meaning or outcome.

Example 2: STEM Design

SCAMPER can easily be applied to any STEM-related issue as students create ideas and solutions for real-world problems. The following examples show how SCAMPER can be used with Science or Engineering content. I also show how the "SCAMPER Stretch" is applied for each:

- ◆ How might we improve the safety of automobiles (what might we substitute, combine, adapt, modify, put to other use, eliminate, or reverse)?
  - – What has been done in the past to improve the safety of homes? Of bicycles? Can we apply these ideas to cars?
  - – Now that we have developed our idea, how might we apply this to improving safety of ___?
- ◆ How might we restore the butterfly population in our community? What do humans need to eliminate? What might we need to minimize, maximize, etc.?
  - – What has been done in the past to restore bird populations? What has been done to restore the population of endangered sharks? Could we adapt these ideas for the butterfly population?
  - – Now that we have developed an idea for the butterfly population, how might this idea be used in another context?
- ◆ What if we apply an element of SCAMPER to the independent variable in the science experiment, what effect will this have?
  - – If we made a similar adjustment with a different scientific question, would we see a similar pattern?

Attributes	Substitute	Combine	Adapt	Modify	Put to Other Use	Eliminate	Reverse
Setting	Substitute for 50 years into the future				Use setting as symbol for character's internal conflict (e.g., storm).		
Conflict				What would make the external conflict (person vs. person) worse? Better?		Take out the reader's understanding of the character's internal conflict (to build suspense).	Shift who "wins" the conflict in the story.
Point of view	Show how the story is different if written from a minor character's point of view.		Adapt to 3rd person limited.				Write the story from the antagonist's point of view.

(Continued)

Attributes	Substitute	Combine	Adapt	Modify	Put to Other Use	Eliminate	Reverse
Tone		Combine both positive and negative tone within a section to show contrast.		Add more language to the character's inner dialogue to enhance the tone.			
Protagonist		What would happen if the protagonist interacts with a protagonist from another famous book?					What if the protagonist had made the opposite decision?

Figure 5.2 SCAMPER +Attributes for Version of a New Story

Source: SCAMPER is from Eberle (2008)

Other Ideas and Tips

◆ SCAMPER can be used to develop solution ideas for characters who experience problems within a story. For example, in what ways might the three little pigs protect themselves from the wolf? What might they substitute, combine, adapt, etc.? How would another character from another book have solved the problem?

◆ SCAMPER can be used to creatively modify a piece of art or music. Innovation is inspired from adapting previous works. For example, what if we reversed the colors scheme in Van Gogh's *Starry Night*? What if we put cardboard to another use to make art? In music, what if we substituted the major key to be a minor key? What effect would it have on the listener?

◆ SCAMPER can be applied as a questioning technique. Questions can be used in any content area to encourage high-level thinking.

  – Math—We must reduce the budget by 20%. How might we adjust the budget using SCAMPER?
  – Social Studies—How did the Ancient Roman Empire "scamperize" from Greek culture (e.g., what did they adapt, maximize, eliminate, etc.)?
  – Science—In what ways might we maximize energy efficiency?
  – Language Arts—Substitute the adjectives in the poem to change the tone.
  – These types of questions can be followed with questions that require students to think through different contexts (e.g., what if this is also applied to ___ situation? How might this idea apply to another context?).

◆ SCAMPER is a go-to strategy for studying inventions. Students can see how various inventions are adapted from previous ideas and products. Students love taking an existing idea (dog collar, coffee mug, shoes, bike helmet) and applying SCAMPER to improve it.

◆ As with many of these strategies, it is important to encourage students to think about their own thinking (metacognition) as they use the strategy. How does this strategy help you think of more ideas? What new insights do you have as a result of using SCAMPER? How do your ideas transfer to other content areas?

Strategy #11: Synectic Trigger Mechanisms

Strategy at a Glance

Synectics involves a number of tools and strategies for deliberately stimulating creative thinking (Gordon, 1961). Much like SCAMPER, Synectic Trigger

Mechanisms (Roukes, 1988) can be used to modify or adapt existing ideas and see old ideas in a new light. The model includes 23 triggers that activate "generative thinking" around a topic or issue. These triggers can serve as transformational thinking prompts for students to explore content with fresh perspectives. Synectic Trigger Mechanisms are used in the business and design fields; however, teachers can use these prompts for encouraging new insight around content, problems, and issues. The following are question prompts for the 23 Synectic Trigger Mechanisms (paraphrased from Roukes, 1988, pp. 15–21):

1. Subtract—What if a part is removed?
2. Repeat—What if a component is repeated?
3. Combine—What if we merge or mix. . . ?
4. Add—What if we expand or add. . . ?
5. Transfer—What if we move this to a new environment or see from a new point of view?
6. Empathize—What if I were this idea/object? How would I feel?
7. Animate—What if we give the idea human qualities?
8. Superimpose—What if we overlay other ideas (disciplines, contexts, point of view, time period)?
9. Changing scale—What if we change the proportion, minimize, or maximize?
10. Substitute—What if we replace. . . ?
11. Fragment—What if we divide it into smaller increments?
12. Isolate—What if we separate or detach the idea?
13. Distort—What if we twist or bend it from its original shape?
14. Disguise—What if we hide or mask. . . ?
15. Contradict—What if we add in the opposite, converse, or reversal?
16. Parody—What if we make fun of the idea (with a pun or joke)?
17. Prevaricate—What if we bend the truth or fictionalize the idea?
18. Analogize—What if we make comparisons to see similarities?
19. Hybridize—What if we cross a __ with ___?
20. Metamorphose—What if we transform the idea or show the idea in a state of change?
21. Symbolize—What if we use a symbol to depict this idea?
22. Mythologize—What if we build a myth around the idea? What if we create an icon?
23. Fantasize—What if we think about bizarre, outlandish, surreal thoughts around this idea?

Example: Science—Engineering to Improve Car Safety

The previous examples provided for SCAMPER can also apply with the Synectic Trigger Mechanisms. Here, I offer additional perspectives using "real student" examples for brainstorming ideas for improving car safety. To support creative thinking, remember to promote a non-evaluative atmosphere where students feel free to share ideas. Crazy ideas are encouraged as they may ignite other more focused ideas. In the idea generation stage, students simply brainstorm various ideas, without critiquing or judging ideas. From these initial ideas, students might create more formal ideas. Even if the ideas listed are not realistic or reasonable, they might inspire creative ideas for marketing or communicating ideas to specific audiences.

◆ Fantasize—What if cars were wrapped in Saran-wrap bubbles?
◆ Repeat—We could add airbags to the back seat or add airbags to extend outwards!
◆ Analogize—A safe car is like a life jacket . . . This makes me think about making the car floatable.
◆ Contradict—What if we removed physical seatbelts to increase safety, replacing them with invisible force shields?
◆ Empathy—If I were a safe car, I would feel proud and protective, like a mother hen protecting unhatched eggs. Is there a way to make protective "shells' for the riders?

These Synectic Trigger Mechanisms can serve as tools for generating a number of ideas (fluency), varied ideas (flexibility), and original ideas (originality) applied to solve problems in the content areas.

Other Tips and Ideas
◆ Use the Synectic Trigger Mechanisms to build creative thinking around how students communicate solutions and ideas (e.g., "How would you sell this idea? How would you persuade others to believe in this idea? How could you communicate this idea to others?").
◆ Use these questions to evoke ideas for creating art or design relevant to the content.
◆ As with SCAMPER, these questions can apply to specific attributes of an item, idea, or problem.
◆ Use these questions after guiding students through the Connections Web (see Chapter 3) so that students can apply innovative thinking to the structure of the content (e.g., "What if we *symbolize* the relationship between matter and energy? What if parts of matter are *distorted*? How does that affect density?")

Strategy #12: SWOT (Evaluating Ideas)

Strategy at a Glance

SWOT is an acronym for Strengths, Weaknesses, Opportunities, and Threats (see Figure 5.3). Often used in the business world, it is used as a strategic planning technique to make decisions while considering various internal (factors within one's control) and external influences (factors outside of one's control) on meeting objectives. In the context of vertical differentiation, it can serve as an evaluation and decision-making tool applied to solution ideas or proposals.

SWOT is similar to de Bono's (1994) PMI (Plusses, Minuses, and Interesting) often used as a high-level thinking strategy in education, but it takes PMI a step further. SWOT provides more layers of challenge by including additional factors (opportunities and threats) that might influence the success of an idea.

Additional complexity can be infused by adding Paul and Elder's (2019) Elements of Thought (implications, assumptions, point of view) within aspects of SWOT:

◆ What are the short- and long-term implications of the strengths and weaknesses?
◆ What assumptions are we making about these opportunities and threats?

	Helpful	Harmful
Internal factors	**Strengths** • How can we leverage strengths? • What benefits do we see?	**Weaknesses** • How can we minimize weaknesses to avoid threats?
External factors	**Opportunities** • What opportunities can we take advantage of? • How can we use strengths to take advantage of opportunities?	**Threats** • What might endanger this idea? • How can we use our strengths to prepare for threats?

Figure 5.3 SWOT Analysis

Source: Adapted from SWOT Analysis Not Simple (2020, October 5). In Wikipedia Commons. https://commons.wikimedia.org/wiki/File:SWOT_Analysis_ssw_1.png

◆ When we consider other stakeholder perspectives (point of view), what can we add to our analysis?

◆ Based on this analysis, what are our next steps?

Example 1: Evaluating New Technologies—Use of Biofuels

In Science, students may learn about alternative energy technologies such as the sustainability of biofuels. Throughout the unit, students might explore the question, "Are biofuels sustainable for the environment?" The teacher might assign groups of students to apply SWOT to first generation biofuels (made from crops), second generation biofuels (made from biomass and agricultural waste), and third generation biofuels (from algae and plants genetically engineered for fuel).

The following example shows SWOT applied to considering possibilities for first generation biofuels to be used as a sustainable fuel source. The internal factors relate to the direct farming of the corn while the external factors are other technological, economic, and societal factors.

You can provide prompts to students to guide their research using the SWOT analysis. How does this biofuel compare to fossil fuels in terms of energy yield, production cost, and greenhouse gas emissions? What are the factors that limit its production? What are the byproducts of the biofuel? See Figure 5.4 for applying SWOT to corn-based ethanol production.

	Helpful	Harmful
Internal factors	**Strengths** • Corn can be regrown • Reduces greenhouse emissions by 13% • Might be profitable for farmers	**Weaknesses** • Corn-based ethanol is difficult to process • Some argue it takes more energy to produce ethanol than it offers as a fuel • Its production is dependent on land, fertilizer, and water for growth
External factors	**Opportunities** • Genetic engineering might be applied to maximize production • By-products such as corn oil result from making ethanol	**Threats** • There's competition with land for other agricultural products (e.g., food to eat) • Cost of food might increase

Figure 5.4 Example of SWOT Applied to Corn-Based Ethanol Production

Each small group can present their SWOT analysis from their research. To take this a step further, students might apply SCAMPER to address threats. For example, how can the biofuel(s) be improved with new technologies? Using your SWOT analysis, which biofuel would you recommend as the most promising for the future?

Example 2: Aesop's Fable- Character Analysis   *Elementary example*

In this example, young students read Aesop's Fable "The North Wind and the Sun" and work in small groups to apply the SWOT analysis to both characters, the Wind and the Sun (see Figure 5.5). The following is an example of SWOT applied to the Wind.

To add more complexity, the teacher might incorporate Elements of Thought (Paul & Elder, 2019): "What are the *assumptions* the Wind has about his strengths and opportunities? What are the *implications* of his weaknesses? How does the Sun perceive the Wind's weaknesses? In order to address the threats, what might the Wind do to win?"

Other Ideas and Tips

- ◆ This strategy can be combined with Six Thinking Hats. First. Students might explore facts, thinking through the white hat. The yellow hat relates to strengths; the black hat relates to weaknesses and threats; the green hat relates to opportunities, while the red hat (emotion) can be applied throughout all aspects. In the end, conclusions can be made about next steps (blue hat).
- ◆ SWOT can be applied to Social Studies content as it applies to studying a historical person or event. For example, if studying a specific president, what were the strengths and weaknesses of the

	Helpful	Harmful
Internal factors	**Strengths** • Ability to create movement • Ability to use powerful force	**Weaknesses** • Can be too powerful if not controlled • Arrogant, prideful
External factors	**Opportunities** • Can blow the man's coat off with power	**Threats** • Excessive force does not always lead to desired results • Can't directly change the man's "choice"

Figure 5.5 SWOT Analysis Applied to the Character, Wind, from Aesop's Fable "The North Wind and the Sun"

President's leadership? What opportunities (given the historical context) did the President have that led to action? What threats interfered with the President's initiatives? Additionally, it might be applied to student thinking through historical events or ideas from perspectives of the time period. For example, "Imagine you were on John F. Kennedy's advisory committee, how would you apply SWOT to the development of the Space Program?"

◆ Any time students develop solution ideas for PBL projects or simulations (e.g., Model United Nations, etc.), students could apply SWOT to their idea to prepare for criticisms and obstacles to their proposed plans.

Strategy #13: Should-Could-Would Criteria

Strategy at a Glance

This strategy is a way for students to consider the usefulness of an idea through developing criteria. It is inspired by what the field of gifted education knows as the litmus test for differentiation: Would, Could, Should. As mentioned in Chapter 1, Harry Passow (1982) posed the questions, "Would all children want to be involved in such learning experiences? Could all children participate in such learning experiences?" Should all children be expected to succeed in such learning experiences? If the answer is yes to any question, then it is likely that the curriculum is not sufficiently differentiated for gifted students.

As I reflect on this litmus test to be applied to gifted curriculum, I realize "would, could, should" are excellent questions for criteria when students debate an issue and evaluate various outcomes applied to curriculum content.

◆ Step 1: Students consider a *should* question. This question presents a focus. What do we need to make a decision about? (Should we ___? Should___ be used?)

◆ Step 2: Students consider *could* questions. These questions relate to implications of the idea (e.g., what this idea might lead to). Could this lead to. . . ? Could this impact. . . ?

◆ Step 3: Students consider *would* questions. These questions relate to the idea's feasibility (would this really work) in achieving a purpose and might also include questions related to different points of view.

When applied to instructional planning, this strategy challenges students to develop appropriate questions to be asked as part of the decision-making process. This presents an opportunity for students to engage in critical thinking by developing criteria and applying it to decision-making as they conduct their research.

Often students are asked to debate or present solution ideas, but this can be taken a step further by asking students to think through perspectives and implications of those ideas. A teacher can use this model informally by asking students to simply think of questions around a topic starting with *should*, *could*, and *would*. More formally, these questions can serve as a frame for research around the topic. This strategy can also be used with a structure for exploring both sides of a "should" issue (see Example 1).

Example 1: Science Study on Genetically Modified Foods

In this example, students study the pros and cons of genetically modified foods, considering if they hold promise for addressing world hunger or if they pose threats to the environment and human health. Students learn that GMO (genetically modified organisms) foods are banned in some parts of the world and develop a controversial question to explore such as, "Should genetically modified foods be banned?" As shown in Figure 5.6, students then pose a number of *could* and *would* questions and sort them for various sides

Should...? What decision needs to be made around the topic?	Should genetically modified foods be banned?	
	Yes	No
Could...? Implications	• Could reducing GMOs lead to better health for consumers? • Could reducing GMOs positively impact the ecosystems, allowing for reduced use of herbicides?	• Could the use of GMOs lead to more nutritious food? • Could the use of GMOs lead to drought-resistant foods which might help the environment?
Would...? Feasibility Perspectives	• Would farmers be able to yield as many crops if GMOs were banned? • Would the amount of food production be sustained without GMO foods?	• Would the use of GMOs help produce more food for people in Third World countries?

Figure 5.6 Should-Could-Would—Genetically Modified Foods Debate

of the argument. As students study more about the topic, they can answer the questions and consider how the evidence weighs into the debate. Students can continue to add more questions as they pursue their research in exploring various perspectives (e.g., ecologists, farmers, consumers).

Example 2: PBL Building a Playground

In this example, as part of a project-based learning project, students are tasked to design a new playground for their school. Additional parameters can be added to make the task more challenging such as meeting a budget, using a variety of simple machines, etc. Before students engage in brainstorming to develop their ideas, students consider criteria by asking should-would-could questions. As shown in Figure 5.7, students would not necessarily debate a *should* question in this instance; they simply brainstorm questions around designing a new playground. This strategy serves as a frame for planning for and making decisions around a project. Asking "What decisions do we need to make?" is an important first step to a planning process. In addition, developing their own questions for decision-making builds self-agency and ignites critical thinking.

Other Tips and Ideas

   ◆   This strategy can work well when thinking through the perspective of a character and decisions that he or she must make. By thinking through a character's internal conflict, students might consider the character's internal voice in thinking through these questions.

Should	• Should we build a new playground or modify the current one? • Should we create a theme for the playground?
Could...? Implications	• Could all students enjoy the playground, including students with physical disabilities? • Could aspects of the playground be too dangerous or could these features provide an appropriate challenge? • Could it withstand weathering over time? • Could parts of the equipment get too hot to play on?
Would...? Feasibility Perspectives	• Would the proposed plan fit the budget? • Would a range of ages consider it to be fun? • Would the old playground equipment be re-used or recycled?

Figure 5.7 Should-Could-Would—PBL on Building a Playground

Elementary Primary

- This strategy can be introduced to younger students by helping them think through their own personal decisions such as owning a new pet (e.g., should I get a new pet?).
- Students could devise a ranking system or matrix to quantify their decisions. For example, they might apply a Likert scale to the questions (on a scale from 1–5), or consider which questions are most important to consider.
- This strategy works well in PBL experiences when students develop a solution to a problem, mock bill, law, proposal, or new invention. Thinking through the various student-generated should-could-would questions will lead to a stronger proposed idea.

Using this strategy does not have to be complicated. You can simply ask, "What decisions need to be made about this topic? Let's consider questions that address controversies (should), implications (could), and feasibility (would)."

6

[handwritten: Metaphors:]
[handwritten: Drowning in work]
[handwritten: couch potato]
[handwritten: heart of gold]

Strategies for Creative Thinking

Making Connections

Creative thinking is intentional thinking that leads to new combinations and new associations of ideas. Creativity involves sensitivity to problems, the ability to generate ideas, thinking in different ways, and the production of novel responses. The previous chapters provided several strategies for being sensitive to problems and generating new ideas. This chapter includes strategies for making connections between ideas, including links between new ideas and existing ideas. These strategies allow students the opportunity to deepen their understanding of content through figurative connections and justify their reasoning for how concepts connect. All the strategies in this chapter provide varied approaches for using the "Metaphorical Thinking" Stretch Prompt (see Figure 6.1).

[handwritten: Dali vs Picasso   Tomatina/Run w Bulls]

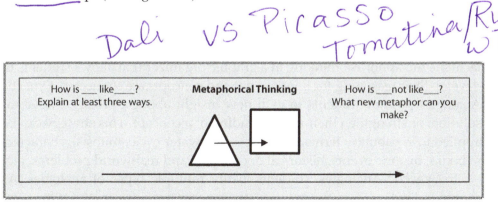

Figure 6.1 Metaphorical Thinking Stretch Prompt

DOI: 10.4324/9781003293286-7

Metaphors and Mental Models

Most of the strategies in this chapter relate to the use of metaphor to strengthen students' deep understanding of knowledge. Metaphors are powerful tools in learning new concepts because they build connections to students' prior knowledge. Through the use of metaphor, we can use students' understanding of familiar concepts to facilitate the development of new learning. These strategies support the construction of mental models. These strategies are not simply "fun" activities that ignite creative thinking (though students do enjoy them!); they support the development of expert-like thinking. As students learn new concepts, their mental models (schemas) are restructured and become more complex.

When students learn something new, their mental models change (Cameron, 2013). Metaphors provide contexts to map the concepts and relationships together, especially in complex learning situations. A metaphor works by providing a schema for connecting new concepts to known concepts (Simpson & Pellegrino, 1993). Basically, metaphors help novices structure the unfamiliar into something familiar. In regard to shaping expertise, novices are known to have more incomplete mental models while experts have rich, elaborate mental models. Studies have shown that the use of metaphor helps novices develop integrative knowledge (e.g., understanding relationships between concepts), changing their mental models to be more organized and complex (Hsu, 2006).

Strategy #14: Synectic Analogies

Strategy at a Glance

Synectics etymologically means "joining together of unrelated elements." In the previous chapter, Synectic Trigger Mechanisms were introduced as a way to generate new ideas. Here, Synectic Analogies (Gordon, 1961) are used to facilitate metaphorical thinking in a graphic organizer that allows students to develop their reasoning for how content and concepts are connected. Synectic Analogies prompt students to gain new insight about a problem, issue, or solution, or strengthen their understanding of a concept. This strategy can be applied to vocabulary terms, processes (e.g., water cycle, mitosis), characters in books, historic events, historical documents, and real-world problems, etc.

In Synectic Analogies, students justify multiple types of analogies. As shown in Figure 6.2, in the first box, the teacher provides an object for comparison (e.g., tree, restaurant, bubble gum, diamond ring, etc.) as a force fit.

Direct Analogy	Personal Analogy
ow is ___ like a _____?	How would it feel to be___?
	I would feel _____ because____.
Contrast Analogy	**New Analogy**
How is ___ not like _____?	_____ is like ___ because_____.

Figure 6.2 Synectic Analogies

Students provide a justifiable response for explaining several ways the content is like the given prompt. Additionally, students apply a personal analogy (how it would feel to be the concept), a contrast analogy (how the concept is not like the same forced fit), and then finally create their own analogy with reasoning. When students engage with various forms of analogy, they have multiple opportunities to elaborate, explain, and justify their reasoning. This process allows for deeper insight about the concept and solidifies new learning. Additionally, this strategy allows for students to construct meaning of concepts by making personal connections between new knowledge and known knowledge.

Example 1: Problem-Based Learning on Monarch Butterfly Population Decline

In this example (Figure 6.3), students develop Synectic Analogies around the decline of butterflies as a way to evoke new ideas and insights for solving the problem. By thinking through these analogies, students not only strengthen their understanding of the problem, but the analogies may evoke new ideas such as "what can we do to change this story? What can be done to prevent the first domino?" allowing students to see the problem from a new perspective.

Example: Math Vocabulary—Place Value

In this example (Figure 6.4), young students elaborate on the concept of place value. Though synectics is used often to enhance creative thinking around a problem and creating solutions, synectics can also strengthen schema as students elaborate and explain the concept through multiple types of analogies. In many ways, this acts as an extension to the Schema Board presented in Chapter 3.

Other Ideas and Tips

◆ Students can complete these analogies as they pursue reading and research around a topic or issue, and then revisit and revise them as they learn new information.

Direct Analogy	Personal Analogy
How is the monarch butterfly decline like a <u>story</u>?	How would it feel to be___?
The monarch butterfly decline is like a story because there are similar patterns. The story of the monarch butterfly starts as "once upon a time" there were so many butterflies that you could hear their wings flap; but one day, the overuse of pesticides affected the milkweed plants. Because of this, there are fewer opportunities for them to reproduce. Pick your ending: the story ends as a tragedy for the butterflies or the story ends as humans intervene to "rescue" them from danger.	*If I were the monarch butterfly, I would feel vulnerable to the decisions made by humans to use pesticides. I would feel I have no control over the situation and worried that there are fewer milkweed plants for my babies to be born.*
Contrast Analogy	**New Analogy**
How is the decline of butterflies not like a <u>story</u>?	____ is like ___ because_____.
The monarch butterfly decline is not like a story because stories are passively experienced by readers. However, the situation with the monarch butterfly is not a set fate but something we may be able to control.	*The monarch butterfly decline is like a series of dominoes falling because the use of pesticides leads to a decrease in milkweed plants (host plants for butterflies) which leads to fewer butterflies being born, which leads to disruption in pollination of plants, which leads to threats in food security.*

Figure 6.3 Synectic Analogies—Monarch Butterfly Decline

- ◆ These analogies work well with abstract concepts such as change, power, structure, truth, perspective, freedom, and also discipline-specific concepts such as democracy, oligarchy, magnetism, velocity, associative property, etc.
- ◆ In Language Arts, the Synectic Analogies can be applied to a character analysis (e.g., how is the character like a boat? etc.)
- ◆ Ask students to reflect on their own thinking after using this strategy. For example, "What new insight do you have about this topic or concept? How do you see the issue differently now?"

good for Math!

Direct Analogy	Personal Analogy
How is place value like a cloud?	How would it feel to be____?
Place value systems are made up of rules according to their base just as clouds form according to "rules" (conditions) in the environment.	*If I were a place value (of the tens), I would feel popular and valuable because I can always be added to others to add "more value" to their present state.*
Place value systems are like clouds because clouds change in form according to how much water is in the clouds (place values change form depending on how many "ones" there are).	
Contrast Analogy	**New Analogy**
How is ____ not like a (same forced fit)?	____ is like ____ because_____.
Place value is not like a cloud because place value was invented by humans, and clouds are formed by nature.	*Place value is like a shelf system because each shelf can only hold a certain amount of "things," then new items have to be placed on the next shelf (place value).*

Figure 6.4 Synectics Analogies—Place Value

Strategy #15: Forced Associations

Strategy at a Glance

This strategy is a variation of Synectic Analogies. Through activities that elicit forced associations, students have opportunities to find new connections between unrelated items. These types of activities, promoting flexible thinking and elaboration, can also be used to generate new solution ideas. A few examples include the following:

◆ Metaphor in a Box—Place various random objects (in a bag or a box) and ask students to make connections between these items and new concepts (see example below: Metaphor in a Box). Students "justify and explain why" the object is representative of the concept or idea. To increase the challenge, ask students to share *three* ways the concept is like the object (this promotes creative fluency and flexibility).

◆ Random Input—can be used to spark ideas around solving a problem or to inspire creative thinking and new insight about a concept or idea. This creative process strategy involves randomly selecting an item (e.g., hammer, doorknob, lamp) or a concrete noun from the dictionary *good for ELA History*

and listing associations or attributes of the word (de Bono, 1992). One approach is to ask students to list the features, function and purpose of this object, and general associations of the object (e.g., this makes me think of . . . reminds me of. . .). Then, connections are made between the content, problem, or issue, and the random item. Various random word generators are available online.

◆ Mix and Match—Students make connections between people and events from different time periods, books, or situations. This provides students with an opportunity to transfer learning across contexts and see patterns through creative thinking. For example:

- Create a dialogue between Dorothy in the *Wizard of Oz* and Harry Potter to discuss how they both confronted the unknown and learned similar life lessons.
- How is the child in the "Emperor's New Clothes" like Henry David Thoreau?
- Imagine Goldilocks was placed in the story of *Little Red Riding Hood*. How would she behave?
- What would the Greek philosopher, Plato, think about this current event (e.g., biotechnology, travel to Mars, global pandemic, etc.)?

Science

Example 1: Metaphor in a Box—Parts of a Cell

In this example, elementary students study the parts of an animal cell. The teacher brings in a box (or bag) that contains objects such as sunglasses, a soda can, map, lightbulb, a rose, rubber band, ring, spoon, a bottle of aloe vera, and a package of salt. Each item is shown to students and placed where all students can see. Then, the teacher lists various parts of the cell on the board: cell wall, nucleus, mitochondria, cell membrane, cytoplasm, vacuole, and ribosomes. Students are asked to make connections between the items and the parts of a cell, justifying how they relate to one another. There is no one right answer, and the cell terms can be associated with more than one item. Students must justify why the cell term relates to one of the objects. The following are possible student responses:

- The vacuole can be represented by the Ziplock bag because it stores extra food, water, or waste.
- The nucleus is symbolized by the map since the nucleus holds directions for other parts of the cell to follow.
- The mitochondria are represented by the spoon because mitochondria changes sugar into energy so the cell can do its job just as a spoon is used to change things into new forms (e.g., egg into a scrambled egg).

This strategy offers opportunities for students to provide justifiable responses. Additionally, the elaboration of the relationship strengthens the development of the student's schema. To provide more challenge, ask students to justify their response with three reasons why they link the term to the object.

Example 2: Random Input for Coral Restoration

In this example, students study threats to coral reefs. Before reading about new trends and research related to restoring coral reefs, students think laterally about the issue by brainstorming ideas and new questions related to understanding the problem. The Random Input method can serve as a tool to generate creative ideas around defined problems.

1. The random word of "suitcase" is selected.
2. Students list features of a suitcase: zippers, pockets, inside pockets, wheels, handle, inside net.
3. Students name the function and purpose of a suitcase: to carry clothing and other items from place to place.
4. Students develop associations with the word suitcase: airports, child suitcases, matching suitcases, luggage fees, excitement of travel, weighing too much, purses, backpacks.

Next, students start relating ideas about the suitcase to coral reef restoration. This is a type of "brainstorming" activity might evoke new questions or ideas that eventually lead to defensible solution ideas. Here are possible student responses during a Random Input brainstorm session:

◆ The idea of matching suitcases makes me wonder if there is a way to clone healthy coral, allowing it to reproduce in new forms.
◆ The idea of zippers makes me think of protection of the items in the suitcase. What can we do to protect the coral reefs? Perhaps we could develop an invisible "zipper" or layer to protect them from invasive species?
◆ The idea that a suitcase carries things from place to place makes me wonder if we can grow new healthy coral in one place and move it to reattach to existing coral.
◆ The idea of being inside a suitcase makes me think of being trapped and suffocating with no air. The coral reefs probably feel suffocated by the acidification (too much carbon dioxide) of the ocean. What can we do to "open" the suitcase?

Table 6.1 Random Input Chart: Random Word:

Features	Function/Purpose	Associations
New Ideas:		

Table 6.1 shows a way to organize student thinking around the Random Input method for generating ideas.

Other Ideas and Tips

- The Metaphor in a Box strategy can also be used to ignite inquiry before teaching a lesson. My colleague, Dr. Vicki Phelps, has shared how such Metaphorical Thinking can be used as a "Mystery Box" before a lesson. Students make predictions or hypotheses of how terms relate to items before learning about the content. Then students conduct research to verify their predictions about their connections (see Mofield & Phelps, 2020). This works especially well for Social Studies content or a pre-reading literature activity (predicting how the items might symbolize various parts of the plot or characters).
- Students can create their own "Metaphor in a Box" to illustrate their understanding of how content relates to the various items.
- Random input can also be used to deepen understanding around content, even if the goal is not to create a solution. For example, students may link how the random word "grain" is related to The Preamble of the Constitution. See Extended Synectics (strategy to follow) for additional ideas of linking features of the content to features of the random word.

Strategy #16: Extended Synectics

Strategy at a Glance

This strategy is a way to develop multiple links between the familiar (what is known) and new content. This is an expansion of Synectic Analogies and

Forced Associations, allowing the student to link multiple parts of a familiar idea to multiple new terms. The steps are as follows:

- ◆ Step 1: Choose a topic or idea that students are familiar with. Ask students to list various parts, features, and associations of this topic. Make a list in column one. Here are examples:
  - – Visiting an amusement park: fast pass, roller coasters, long lines, cotton candy, ticket booth, train, tram, water rides, etc.
  - – Eating lunch at a cafeteria: waiting in line, choosing entree, silverware station, drink station, tray, milk, paying the cashier, etc.
  - – Shopping at a grocery store: produce aisle, freezer section, food samples, self-checkout, deli, bakery, floral section, shopping cart, etc.
- ◆ Step 2: Ask students to list vocabulary or new learning from the current unit in Column 2.
- ◆ Step 3: Ask students to make connections between any word in Column 2 to any word in Column 1. How is ___(new learning) like any part of Column 1? Draw arrows between the columns to guide students to see the links that are made. Ask students to justify their responses and explanations.

Extended Synectics works well as a short review of concepts, providing students with the opportunity to elaborate on the connections they are making. This strategy is more challenging than simple force-fit analogies (e.g., how is an independent variable like a lamp?) because it allows students to examine multiple facets of an idea and how they operate together within a system. This allows for more complexity as students can relate new content to a familiar topic in the context of how parts interact within a system.

Example 1: Science Experiments

In this example (see Figure 6.5), students are learning about the scientific method. The teacher asks students to list what they see or know about playing on a playground (Column 1). Then, the teacher asks students to list important terms, facts, and ideas from learning about applying the scientific method to science experiments (Column 2).

Students might make the following connections (though there are many different possible responses):

- ◆ The independent variable is like one side of the seesaw. Just as a force from one side of the seesaw causes the other side to move,

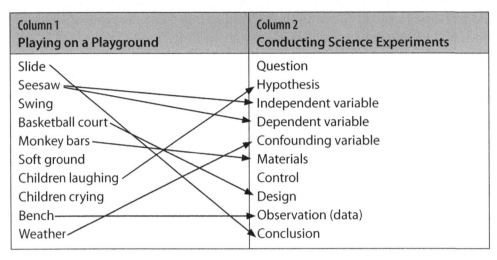

Figure 6.5 Extended Synectics: Science Experiments and Playgrounds

an independent variable will cause something a change in the dependent variable.

◆ The dependent variable is like the other side of the seesaw. It is the observed result of the weight on the other end.

◆ A hypothesis is like an expectation of what we think will happen on the playground: children will be laughing.

◆ A confounding variable is like the weather, another variable that might influence the delight of children.

◆ Materials are like monkey bars. Each material is used in a certain way in a certain order just as a person goes through the monkey bars in order.

◆ The design is like a basketball court. There are clear parameters and procedures spelled out in advance to follow.

◆ Observations relate to the bench. Just as care-givers watch their children, scientists observe the changes or details in their experiment.

◆ The conclusion is like the slide: after conducting the experiment (climbing the ladder), evaluating observations (at the top of the slide) a scientist arrives at a conclusion (goes down the slide) to report what was observed.

Example 2: Ancient Egypt

In this example (see Figure 6.6), a Social Studies teacher asks a group of students to list terms, concepts, and ideas associated with what they know about growing a garden. Next, the teacher reviews key terms and ideas related to a

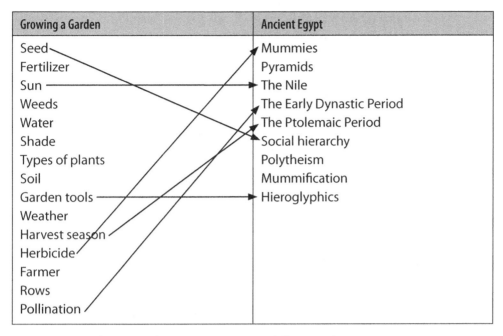

Growing a Garden	Ancient Egypt
Seed	Mummies
Fertilizer	Pyramids
Sun	The Nile
Weeds	The Early Dynastic Period
Water	The Ptolemaic Period
Shade	Social hierarchy
Types of plants	Polytheism
Soil	Mummification
Garden tools	Hieroglyphics
Weather	
Harvest season	
Herbicide	
Farmer	
Rows	
Pollination	

Figure 6.6 Extended Synectics: Science Experiments and Playgrounds

unit on Ancient Egypt. The teacher then asks students to explain how aspects of Ancient Egypt are like growing a garden.

Students might make the following connections (though there are many different possible responses):

◆ Hieroglyphics are like garden tools. Hieroglyphics were "tools" for communication to spread ideas, as garden tools are used to spread and cultivate the soil.
◆ Social hierarchy relates to different types of seeds planted in various rows in the garden. In Ancient Egypt there were different types of social classes, each with specific roles and functions, just as in a garden, there are different types of seeds planted in separate rows, each with specific structures and growth patterns.
◆ Polytheism in Ancient Egypt relates to weather. In Ancient Egypt they worshipped many different gods used to explain why things happen (e.g., why the Nile rises), just as various types of weather (good and bad) lead to explanations for why a garden can flourish or fail.
◆ Mummies relate to herbicides in a garden. Mummification was a process to preserve bodies, protecting them from dry air, chemicals,

and other factors that influence decay, just as herbicides can be used to protect plants from outside threats like weeds.

◆ The Nile is like the sun. The Nile was central to Egyptian farming and overall way of life, just as the sun is the central source of energy transfer to the plant and its overall production of vegetables.

◆ The Early Dynastic Period is like the pollination of plants in the garden because this period involved the unification of upper and lower kingdoms, just as in pollination there is a bringing together of pollen grains from one plant to another.

◆ The Ptolemaic Dynasty is like a fall harvest. This was one of the later dynasties. During this period, trade flourished, just as there is an abundance of "fruit" in the fall harvest.

Extended Synectics Variation: House-Tree-Person

This strategy is inspired by the famous House-Tree-Person psychology projective test (Buck, 1970). Rather than it being used to understand a person psychologically, building metaphors around a house, a tree, or a person can be an engaging way for students to think about the relationships of concepts through a visual representation.

The steps are as follows:

◆ Step 1: Ask students to draw a house, a tree, or a stick figure (person)

◆ Step 2: Ask students to show how the concept or idea (e.g., a persuasive essay, erosion, The Constitution, an atom) is like a house, a tree, or a person, specifically how the "parts" are related to the functions.

◆ Step 3: Ask follow-up questions about how the concept or idea develops:
  – House: How is the house built? (e.g., how was the *constitution* built?)
  – Tree: How does the tree grow? (e.g., how does *erosion* grow?)
  – Person: What makes the person thrive? (e.g., what makes a *persuasive essay* thrive?)

This strategy works well with a concept that includes multiple parts or an idea that is abstract such as "truth" or "power." You may recommend students labeling how the concept specifically is like the specific parts on the house, tree, or person. For example, students might label the following to relate concepts:

◆ House: foundation, door, windows, roof, bricks, mortar
◆ Tree: roots, trunk, branches, leaves, fruit
◆ Person: head, mouth, heart, hands, feet, legs

In the following example, a student response shows how components of a persuasive essay are related to a tree:

◆ Roots: understanding the audience
◆ Trunk: the main claim
◆ Branches: various arguments and points to defend the claim
◆ Leaves: types of persuasive devices or tools
◆ Fruit: the intended effect the message has on the audience

How does a persuasive essay grow/thrive? A persuasive essay fully develops when the claim addresses the needs of the audience and is the fullest when there are strong, sufficient, and relevant arguments to defend the thick trunk, the claim. The stronger the argument with sufficient ethos, pathos, and logos appeals, the thicker and more developed the tree will be.

Other Ideas and Tips

◆ To create additional opportunities for challenge, ask students to connect how a vocabulary term may be the opposite of a word from the familiar column. For example, the Nile is the opposite of shade for a garden, because shade prevents growth, but the Nile allowed for Egypt to flourish.

◆ Though it would not allow students to connect content to a "system," students enjoy making connections between new content and types of candy (e.g., ask students to name their favorite types of candy and list this in Column 1).

◆ As students make connections between Column 2 and Column 1, they will often think of new ideas to add to Column 1(the familiar) to better fit an analogy.

Strategy #17: Metapatterns

Strategy at a Glance

Metapatterns noted by Bateson (1979) are "patterns of patterns" found universally in nature, architecture, politics, and many other aspects of society. Tyler Volk describes them as "functional universals for forms in space, processes in time, and concepts in mind" (1995, p. ix). Metapatterns allow for analyzing the interrelated aspects of systems, their parts, and their contexts. When students are taught to look for Metapatterns in various content areas, it provides a way of organizing questions and research and allows them to see overarching connections across disciplines (Volk & Bloom, 2007).

Connecting content to universal themes such as change, patterns, and systems is often used in gifted education curriculum (e.g., Vanderbilt Programs for Talented Youth curriculum units: see Stambaugh & Mofield, 2018; William and Mary curriculum units: see College of William and Mary/Center for Gifted Education, 2008). Metapatterns are indeed related to this idea, though they offer additional layers of complexity as students explore big ideas and patterns within the content they study.

The following is a list of some of the Metapatterns described by Volk (Volk, 1995; Volk & Bloom, 2007):

1. Spheres: form allows for maximum volume with minimum surface; serves to contain or protect (domes, planets, eggs)
2. Sheets: the function of flatness allows for maximum transfer of matter, energy, or information; sheets maximize contact (leaf, solar collectors)
3. Tubes: structure allows for transport (often from sheets and spheres), connection, and support; provide paths for transporting long distances efficiently (electric circuits, interstate highways, leaf veins)
4. Webs: connect parts within systems, often consisting of centers or clusters (systems of the human body, ecosystems, social hierarchies)
5. Borders: function to protect; openings allow for controlled exchange (cell wall, eggshell, rules in society)
6. Binaries: two opposites come together to unify and make efficient; other patterns include binaries as conflict (protons and neutrons, male and female, veins and arteries, multiplication and division)
7. Centers: allow for a system to be stable; a "code" that connects the whole of the parts provides cohesion to the parts (queen bee, DNA, nucleus of an atom or cell; societal core texts such as the Magna Carta)
8. Layers: provide organization to a system through levels of successive systems. Includes hierarchies, holarchies (worlds within worlds), nested systems, or stratification to allow a system to be stable (layers of the atmosphere, onions, Ancient Egypt pyramids and society)
9. Breaks: sudden changes in a system; a breakthrough the border of a system; discontinuity (metamorphosis, political revolution, waterfalls, fight or flight response, epiphanies, stages in science, development, etc.)
10. Cycles: recurring patterns in systems over time (rock cycle, carbon cycle, hero's journey, planetary orbits, chord sequence in music)

See Volk and Bloom (2007) for additional Metapatterns: gradients, triggers, arrows, emergence, holons, clonons.

Throughout a unit of study, students can look for Metapatterns using a Metapattern Map (see Resource 6.1; downloadable at www.routledge.com/9781032275581). In addition, you may use the following

Metapattern Map

Spheres: contain, protect	Sheets and tubes: transfer and transport	Webs: connected relationships
Borders: boundaries	Centers: provides stability	Binaries: natural pairs
Layers: organized levels	Cycles: repeated patterns	Breaks: sudden change

Resource 6.1 Metapattern Map

Source: Metapatterns are described in Volk, T. (1995) Metapatterns: Across space, time, and mind. Columbia University Press.

question prompts to guide students to make connections across patterns and create generalizations.

- How do tubes connect to sheets and spheres?
- What causes breaks in the boundaries and cycles?
- How does the center hold together the web?
- How do spheres function to protect layers or webs?
- How do layers and centers provide stability to the system?

Example 1: Metapatterns in Ecology

In this example, students study ecosystems in science. Throughout the unit, students are asked to keep a Metapattern Map (see Figure 6.7) to record patterns they notice throughout the unit, with a goal to understand the form and function of structures within ecology.

Students may add to their maps over the course of the unit. To further deepen students' understanding of the content, students might study how these patterns are related to one another (much like the Connections Web in Chapter 2). Students can draw arrows across the Metapatterns to show connections. This is especially important in guiding students to understand how the content operates as a system. For example, students might connect centers, breaks, and webs (a break in center will dismantle the web). Students can then reflect on major insights or generalizations from examining content through the lens of Metapatterns. For example, students might realize when boundaries of ecosystems overlap, the dysfunction of one ecosystem can disrupt another ecosystem.

Example 2: Metapatterns and Archetypes in Literature

In this example, students apply Metapatterns to Hans Christian Andersen's short story, "The Emperor's New Clothes." Students may be learning about various story patterns in literature (e.g., hero's journey, character arcs, plot structure). Metapatterns provide another abstract perspective at examining these patterns. The following are examples of some Metapatterns students might notice in the story:

- Sphere: the society is functioning within a sphere of pretense. The individuals in the story feel protected (from ridicule) when they are pretending.
- Sheets and tubes: the invisible thread/clothing serves as a sheet. Because it is an invisible sheet, it maximizes characters' exposure to the truth (which emphasizes the theme).

Spheres: contain, protect	Sheets and tubes: transfer and transport	Webs: connected relationships
The biosphere is the global ecosystem consisting of biotic and abiotic factors.	Producers (plants) have leaves that are "sheets" to maximize how much energy it takes in. Food webs show invisible "tubes" of energy transported within a food chain.	The food web is the connection of consumers and resources, illustrating the flow of energy.
Borders: boundaries	**Centers: provides stability**	**Binaries: natural pairs**
Some ecosystems have boundaries, though many overlap. Some zones include land zone, transition zone, and aquatic zone.	Keystone species are species that other species depend on- if removed the ecosystem is disrupted.	Balance of biotic and abiotic factors interacting Predators and prey Mutualism
Layers: organized levels	**Cycles: repeated patterns**	**Breaks: sudden change**
The food web consists of various levels: autotrophs, herbivores, primary carnivores, secondary carnivores. Organization of ecology: organism, population, community, ecosystem, biosphere	The Nitrogen Cycle- Nitrogen is converted to nitrates by nitrogen-fixing bacteria (found in soil). Plants use nitrates to make amino acids, humans and animals eat plants (amino acids build muscle); when plants and animals die, bacteria convert nitrates back to nitrogen gas into the atmosphere.	Breaks in a food web caused by an invasive species or the loss of a species leads to loss of other species and an imbalanced ecosystem.

Figure 6.7 Metapattern Map: Ecosystems

Source: Metapatterns are from Volk (1995)

- ◆ Center: pride is at the center of keeping everyone from speaking truth. If people did not worry about appearing stupid, then the system of lying would be disrupted.
- ◆ Borders: the society is functioning within the border/boundary of the king's approval.
- ◆ Break: the breakthrough occurs when the child reveals the truth.
- ◆ Cycle: in this story, there is a cycle of pretending which leads to more pretending. This repeated pattern is only broken when the child reveals the truth.
- ◆ Binary: truth vs. perception

Finding these Metapatterns gives students an opportunity to think more abstractly about the story. These can also be paired with learning about archetypes in stories (broad patterns more specific to literature).

- ◆ Character archetypes (the innocent, the hero, the sage) have core values and fears (center) that motivate their thoughts and behaviors. These characters operate with their own personality boundaries (borders), influencing how they interact with other characters (web).
- ◆ Situation archetypes are specific patterns (cycles) in stories (e.g., unhealable wound, initiation, quest, good vs. evil) that lead to "breaks" in the story.
- ◆ Symbolic archetypes (colors, circles, class, darkness) may symbolize various Metapatterns (e.g., binary of light vs. dark).

Other Ideas and Tips

- ◆ Students can complete independent learning projects through the lens of Metapatterns. Some websites (e.g., https://metapatterns. wikidot.com/) showcase various samples of student work linking topics to Metapatterns.
- ◆ When introducing the concept of Metapatterns, ask students to go on a Metapattern scavenger hunt, noting examples in a journal the various Metapatterns they see throughout a day (e.g., putting on suntan lotion serves as a sheet; the straw in my drink is a tube to transfer liquid to my mouth; wearing a face mask creates a border between my personal germs and others').
- ◆ To emphasize cross-curricular connections, develop a bulletin board focused on Metapatterns, showing examples of spheres, binaries, sheets and tubes, etc. in content studied throughout the year. This might also include current events.

◆ Volk and Bloom (2007) present various icons for Metapatterns that can be used to facilitate thinking. Alternatively, you may ask students to develop their own symbols for each Metapattern.

◆ Students can use Metapatterns to better understand and examine problems. For example, in considering the problem of environmental threats to coral reefs through Metapatterns, students can identify the connectedness of coral reefs within their ecosystems (e.g., algae, temperature) to determine what causes the break within the system.

◆ Use the Connections Web (see Chapter 3) or hexagonal thinking to list examples of Metapatterns and to guide students to understand how they are interconnected.

◆ I've noticed that many teachers initially see this strategy as "too deep" or "too abstract," but in my experience working with gifted students, I see they absolutely love finding these patterns! Gifted students often demonstrate insightful connections and see patterns and similarities across multiple concepts. Metapatterns provide the organizational structure for students to demonstrate these insightful connections. Don't be afraid to expose students to this type of thinking.

7

Strategies for Constructing Arguments

Throughout this text, I have emphasized the importance of providing opportunities for students to justify their reasoning and arrive at valid conclusions. When we ask students to "justify, explain why" either in a small group discussion or a formal essay, we desire for students to provide a logical, reasonable explanation, rooted in evidence, and linked to their claim. As a former English Language Arts teacher, I noticed that students could easily cite evidence; yet, they often needed support in articulating how evidence related to their reasoning, or sometimes they jumped to conclusions without adequate explanation. Structures are needed to facilitate student thinking. This chapter focuses on the "Argument" Stretch Prompt (Figure 7.1) with strategies to support how students use reasoning to construct their own logical arguments.

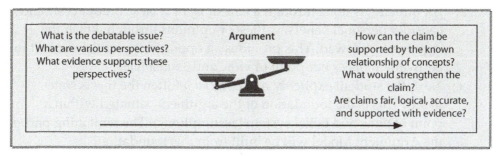

What is the debatable issue? What are various perspectives? What evidence supports these perspectives?	**Argument**	How can the claim be supported by the known relationship of concepts? What would strengthen the claim? Are claims fair, logical, accurate, and supported with evidence?

Figure 7.1 Argument Stretch Prompt

DOI: 10.4324/9781003293286-8

Maybe for AP IV writing

he models that follow can also be used for students to critically examine
ıments of others by evaluating how claims of an author can be improved
or strengthened. You may ask, "How might the reasoning and logic be
improved? What flaws do we see in these arguments?" Thus, it is important
to use these models not only to construct arguments but to analyze them.
These strategies work hand in hand with Paul and Elder's (2019) Intellectual
Standards discussed in Chapter 2.

Strategy #18: Argument Construction Model

Strategy at a Glance

This strategy goes beyond teaching the typical essay structure of writing an
argument essay. Students are often taught to create an introductory paragraph
with a thesis, support the thesis with points and evidence, and then provide
a conclusion. In the Argument Construction Model, more attention is given
to *how* the reasoning of the argument is constructed. This strategy serves as a
model for thinking about how an argument is built, much like constructing a
building. Elements of Thought (from Paul & Elder, 2019) are used as building
blocks for the argument structure (see Figure 7.2 and Figure 7.3 and Resource
7.1 downloadable at www.routledge.com/9781032275581).

1. All thinking is done around *concepts*. First, ask students to identify
   the main concepts associated with the question at hand and then
   think about how those concepts connect. These concepts can be
   written on the blocks. These are the ideas that will formulate all reasoning. These "blocks" or concepts might be used multiple times in
   the argument construction and can fit anywhere within the model. It
   is important to guide students to identify the concepts used in their
   thinking as they formulate their argument.
2. All thinking is done through a lens or *point of view*. Students should
   consider personal beliefs, values, or opinions through which the
   argument is viewed. This provides an opportunity for the student to
   be aware of his or her point of view and *assumptions*.
3. Next, the student explicitly makes a *claim* (often the thesis statement). This is the foundation of the argument, situated within a
   point of view and belief system (assumptions). The remaining part of
   the Argument Model will be built from this foundation.
4. Then the writer plans at least 3 reasons why the claim is valid. These
   reasons (with evidence) are pre-planned and noted on the walls of

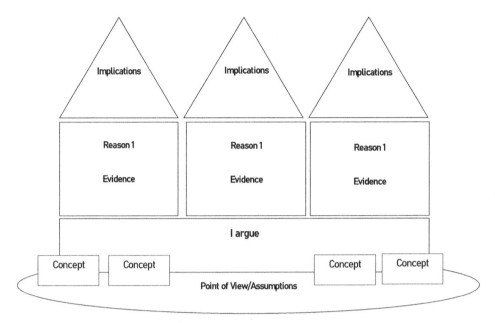

Figure 7.2 Argument Construction Based on Paul's Elements of Thought

Source: Based on Paul and Elder (2019) Elements of Reasoning

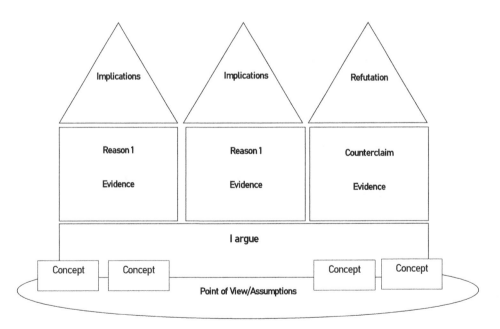

Figure 7.3 Argument Construction with Counterclaim

Source: Based on Paul and Elder (2019) Elements of Thought the building. The student cites evidence and provides reasons for how the evidence supports the claim.

5. Complexity is added by including additional explanations of the given reasons by explaining *"implications"* (what could happen as a result of the reason/evidence described). These implications or effects enhance the argument and are added as roofs (though it is not always necessary for all major reasons to include implications).

6. In the Argument Construction Model with Counterclaim, a *counterargument* can also be addressed and refuted (see Figure 7.3).

Once the argument is built, it can be applied to various structures of writing. This model is meant to guide thinking around how an argument is logically constructed and organized. Figure 7.4 shows how this model can be used with student-friendly prompts. These models may be used as a visual in the classroom for students to refer to during discussion or when planning a formal essay.

Example 1: Should Switchgrass Ethanol Replace Fossil Fuels?
In this example, students have been researching the potential for switchgrass (a deep-rooted perennial grass) to replace the use of fossil fuels in the future. Using their research and sources, students prepare to write a valid argument.

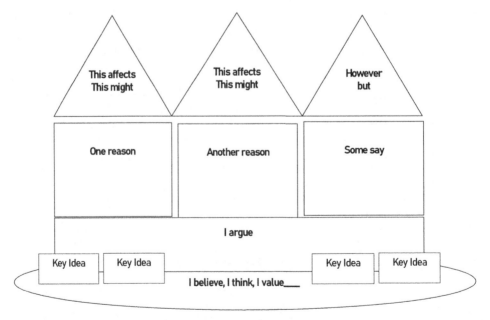

Figure 7.4 Argument Construction with Student-Friendly Prompts

Source: Based on Paul and Elder (2019) Elements of Thought

- Concepts: *sustainability, dependency, environment, renewable and non-renewable resources, power, scarcity, economy.* Arguments can be made by articulating the relationship between these concepts.
- Point of view/assumptions: I believe we should decrease dependency on fossil fuels to take care of the environment. I am aware of my environmentalist perspective.
- Claim: switchgrass ethanol is a *sustainable* solution for replacing fossil fuels, decreasing our *dependency* on non-renewable resources.
- Reasoning 1: switchgrass is a perennial crop (renewable resource) that can grow quickly and in various conditions (prairies, marshes, woods).
- Implications 1: because switchgrass can be grown year after year, this eliminates dependency on non-renewable resources.
- Reasoning 2: switchgrass can be grown on non-fertile land.
- Implications 2: because it can be grown on non-fertile land, it will not compete with land that grows food crops, eliminating the "land for food vs. fuel" debate.
- Counterclaim: some may argue that this does not yield profitable biomass per acre.
- Refutation: however, the technology to produce higher yields is relatively new and can likely be addressed with new technologies in the future.

Students can also explain other reasons to support the claim. For example, Reasoning 3: Switchgrass is beneficial to the environment by preventing soil erosion. Implications 3: By preventing soil erosion (keeping soil in its place), it provides a habitat to other wildlife. The structure is flexible so that multiple walls (reasons/evidence) can be added.

Example 2: Should We Have a Vending Machine in Our School?

Young students are introduced to developing arguments and are asked if they think vending machines (with candy) should be allowed in their school.

The teacher conducts a quick debate in which students stand on either side of the room to represent their perspective. As each student shares his or her point of view, the teacher "makes thinking visible" by constructing the arguments on the board (one argument for vending machines and another argument against vending machines), guiding students to use concept connections within their arguments (example concepts: choice, power, control, health, profit, protection, responsibility). This allows both sides of the room to see the two arguments and how they are constructed, along with the concepts, point of view, and implications of each argument. This approach allows students to go beyond a quick debate where they simply share initial opinions on a topic. Through thinking through the elements of argument construction, student opinions are shaped into logically supported claims.

Other Ideas and Tips

◆ Students can engage in quick debates (stand on one side of the room to argue X vs. Y) and refer to the structure of the "Techniques for Argument Structures" (see the end of this chapter) diving in deeper into their reasoning with implications beyond citing evidence.

◆ These structures are also useful in analyzing how other authors develop their claims with reasoning. This tool can be used as a graphic organizer to help students understand the organization of arguments in various texts.

Strategy #19: Balloon Debate

Strategy at a Glance

The balloon debate is a popular activity that provides students opportunities to generate a number of persuasive arguments as they imagine themselves in a hot air balloon with others (Sather, 1999). The catch is that the hot air balloon is too heavy and is sinking. All people in the balloon must be "thrown off" except for one person in order to keep the hot air balloon from plummeting. Each student (assigned as a person, event, or idea to defend) presents a short argument (2 minutes or less) for why he or she should not be thrown out of the balloon. This evokes creative thinking by eliciting multiple and flexible responses, and critical thinking by requiring students to construct valid, logical arguments.

Multiple versions of the balloon debate exist. The basic steps of a typical balloon debate include the following:

1. Assign five to six students to take part in a debate around a specific issue, assigning a role to each student (e.g., a character, historical figure, invention idea, event, place). Provide students with time to gather data, make inferences, and consider short- and long-term implications of their idea. They may use the "Argument Construction Model" (previous strategy) to plan their arguments.

2. Debate Round 1: Explain the situation "You are all in the hot air balloon, but it is too heavy and is starting to sink. We will have to throw all but one of you out. You have 2 minutes to explain why you should stay in the balloon."

3. Each student takes turns explaining why he or she should stay in the balloon.

4. Debate Round 2: The teacher asks one question to each student to dive further into the content of their argument. For example:
   a) What makes your contribution so special?
   b) What are the long-term effects of___?
   c) What concepts are you using in your argument and how are they connected?
   d) In what ways might you provide a rebuttal to someone else's argument (e.g., "___ said, but I disagree because___")
   e) Can you elaborate on ____ part in your speech?

5. Round 3: Students provide a summary of their most pressing points (one last word).

6. The audience (other students) vote to determine which person should stay in the balloon. The decision must be based on the arguments given (students should not necessarily vote for their "favorite" character). Be sure to ask students to select and explain the criteria they used to determine their decisions.

Here are a few examples of questions that might be posed in various content areas for a balloon debate:

good for Cadet cornerstone

- Which invention in the Industrial Revolution had the greatest impact?
- Which of the 13 colonies should new colonists be persuaded to move?
- Which ancient civilization had the most influence on the modern world?
- Which math formula is the most useful in everyday life?
- Which piece of art should be named the most significant?
- Which living thing is most important to the ecosystem?
- Which chapter (from the book) is the most important to the character's development?
- Which Egyptian leader had the most significant impact on Egyptian civilization (works for any leader and civilization)?

Example: Most Significant Piece of Art

In this example, students are assigned a piece of art to research (e.g., *Starry Night* by Van Gogh, *Mona Lisa* by da Vinci, *The School of Athens* by Raphael, *Christina's World* by Wyeth, and *The Sleeping Gypsy* by Rousseau). They take time to prepare notes about the artist and why the given art is significant (and, therefore, should not be thrown out of the balloon). They are also given time to

good for upper level art

research aspects of the others' art to prepare more informed arguments. Each student presents his or her argument for up to 2 minutes. Then, in Round 2, as a variation, instead of the teacher asking prepared questions, the audience asks the "artists" questions related to their given speeches. In Round 3, each artist explains why his or her work is better compared to the person to the left (e.g., Van Gogh explains why his art is more significant than da Vinci's). The teacher guides students in a discussion to determine what criteria should be made about choosing who should stay in the balloon. A vote is made for who presented the most persuasive argument for not being thrown out of the balloon.

Other Ideas and Tips

◆ Provide additional structure for the debate each round by first asking students to focus on positive aspects of their character/idea (Round 1), then ask students to discuss how their accomplishments compare to others in the balloon (e.g., the person to their left) (Round 2).

◆ Pose the balloon debate in a tournament style. For example, form two hot air balloons with four students each. In Round 1, person 1 and person 2 (within one balloon) debate against each other, and one is voted "out." The winner then goes against the winner of one of the pairs in the second balloon. This is repeated for the second pair in each balloon.

◆ To involve more of the audience, in the second round, ask volunteers from the audience to create additional arguments for defending a person in the balloon. Each person in the balloon can then have one last opportunity to present a summary of their argument.

◆ Encourage students to form logical arguments using a specific argument structure (see the following sections in this chapter).

Techniques for Argument Structures

We often ask students to defend or argue for a point of view, but arguments are more powerful when students learn structures for doing so. Whether defending a stance in a four-corner debate, a Tug of War debate, or writing a persuasive essay, students can be taught sophisticated structures for presenting reasoned arguments. It is important for students to be taught _multiple_ ways to construct valid, logical arguments with critical reasoning, as this flexibility will prepare them for defending ideas in various fields and disciplines. When students present arguments, they are not just stating _what_ they know, but _how_ they know it, with evidence and evaluation of this evidence. When students are taught these argument structures, they can move from simple use of evidence to more sophisticated elaboration of reasoning.

Classical/Aristotelian Argument

Philo chairs

The Classical/Aristotelian argument is used to persuade an audience to adopt a stance. Its structure is based on the development of ethos, logos, and pathos rhetorical appeals as modes of persuasion. These work well for audiences who are "fence-sitters" who might be persuaded towards a particular stance. The goal of this type of argument is to "win" the fence sitter over.

- Ethos appeals refer to developing credibility and trust
- Logos appeals refer to developing and supporting logical reasoned claims
- Pathos appeals refer to appealing to the emotions of the audience

The basic structure of a classical or Aristotelian argument is as follows (adapted from Purdue OWL, n.d.a):

- Introduction
  - *Exordium*: An introduction or hook. Provides ethos (credibility)
  - *Narratio*: Provides background of the topic
  - *Proposito* and *Partito*: Thesis—Presents a logical claim- what is being argued (logos)
- Body
  - *Confirmato*: Evidence to support claims (logos)
  - *Refutatio*: Evidence for counterarguments
- Conclusion
  - Summary of evidence presented
  - *Peroratio*: Provides final appeal (pathos) for claim. Offers a solution (call to action)

Rogerian Argument

Based on the work of Carl Rogers (a psychotherapist), Rogerian arguments rely on cooperation and are used to show a middle ground between two very different viewpoints. The aim is to arrive at a mutually acceptable solution for both sides. These arguments work well in conflict resolution because they lead to compromised alternatives. The argument is based on telling the audience (e.g., opposing view) they are understood, show validation of the other side's position, and show how both sides share similar qualities and goals. This builds credibility (ethos) in allowing the opposing side to trust you.

Rogerian arguments do not have to follow a specific linear structure. The outline here shows one way it can be approached (adapted from Purdue Online Writing Lab, n.d.b):

- Introduction: Introduce the topic or the problem.
- Opposing View: Explain you understand the view and goal of the other side.
- Context for Opposing View: Explain you see the opposing side has a valid point. (You have a good point. Sometimes. . .)
- Introduce Your Stance: Explain how your viewpoint is different from the other side.
- Context for Your Position: Explain how your position is valid in various situations.
- Benefits: Explain how the opposition will benefit if they use elements of your position.

Example: Video Game Arguments

As a class activity, students could defend a similar claim (e.g., video games are harmful or helpful) using various structures. As students state these arguments, audience members can compare the impact of the structures on the message and persuasive effects. Students can discuss how different argument structures may work better in some situations for particular audiences compared to others. An example of video game arguments is presented in two structures (each arguing a different stance).

Classical/Aristotelian Argument: Video Games are Harmful

- Introduction
  - *Exordium*: An introduction or hook. Provides ethos (credibility)
  - According to Statistica (n.d.), "the average time spent playing video games is 7.71 hours per week in the US."
  - *Narratio*: Provides background of the topic
    - Playing video games is a part of life for most children, yet it can be highly addictive.
  - *Proposito* and *Partito*: Thesis- Presents a logical claim- what is being argued (logos)
    - Video games are harmful to children.
- Body
  - *Confirmato*: Evidence to support claims (logos)
    - Leads to aggressive behavior (cite sources and specific facts)
    - Can be addictive because of the release of dopamine (cite sources and specific facts)
    - Leads to too much "screen time" (cite sources and specific facts)
  - *Refutatio*: Evidence for counterarguments
    - Though some might argue that there is no clear cause-effect relationship between video games and violence, 90% of pediatricians indicate they believe there is a link.

- ◆ Conclusion
    - – Summary of evidence presented
    - – *Peroratio*: Provides final appeal (pathos) for claim. Offers a solution (call to action)
        - • Clearly, limits should be made on the use of video games so they are not harming the health and future of children's lives.

Rogerian Argument: Video Games are not Harmful

- ◆ Introduction: Introduce the topic or the problem.
    - – Children love to play video games in their free time. Some parents are concerned about how it might negatively affect children.
- ◆ Opposing View: Explain you understand the view and goal of the other side.
    - – Parents are concerned that children could easily spend too much time on these games; they are addictive, and sometimes include violent content.
- ◆ Context for Opposing View: Explain you see how opposing viewpoints can be valid. (You have a good point. Sometimes. . .)
    - – It is true that if left unmonitored, children can spend too many hours playing video games instead of playing outside with their friends or working on their homework. Research does in fact indicate that about 8% of children are addicted to video games.
- ◆ Introduce Your Stance: Explain how your viewpoint is different from the other side.
    - – However, generally speaking, video games are not harmful to children. Children enjoy playing with their friends on video games which helps their social skills. Video games can also improve attention and concentration, even enhancing multitasking skills.
- ◆ Context for Your Position: Explain how your position is valid in various situations.
    - – There is research to show that in many situations, children enhance their reasoning and problem-solving abilities when they play video games.
- ◆ Benefits: Explain how the opposition will benefit if they use elements of your position.
    - – Perhaps parents can create time limits for the amount of time children spend playing video games and monitor closely the content so that children can enjoy this time and even build their reasoning skills!

Other Tips and Ideas

◆ Add complexity to typical short class quick debates (such as "Tug of War" thinking routine; Project Zero, 2019) by using argument structures. For example, students typically write pieces of evidence (on sticky notes) to support a claim for one side of an argument and place it on one side of a visual rope for a visual "Tug of War." Beyond writing this evidence, students can write additional elements (from Paul's Elements of Thought, rhetorical appeals, implications, etc.) and organize the elements into one of the structured arguments on the "Tug of War" visual rope.

◆ As students develop their arguments, ask them to assess their arguments using Paul and Elder's (2019) Intellectual Standards (see Chapter 2). For example, students should consider the clarity, accuracy, relevance, precision, depth, breadth, logic, significance, and fairness of their thinking.

◆ Introduce other models for argumentation (e.g., Toulmin argument, proposal argument) to add even more complexity for older students.

Supporting Expression of Arguments

To support students' expression of analyzing and articulating arguments, you can provide sentence frames for reasoning (see Figure 7.5). These stems can reduce the cognitive load of *how* to "say it the right way" allowing students to focus their thinking on *what* to argue. These can be posted on a bulletin board for easy student reference.

• The reason I think this is because_____.
• If we know _____, then we can figure out_____.
• I question the credibility of_____ because_____.
• I am going to argue _____ because_____.
• Some might see this differently, though. Some might argue that_____.
• The positive things about this are___. The negative things are___.
• This might lead to_____ which might lead to___.
• There's a fine line, though, between ___ and ___.

Figure 7.5 Sentence Frames for Reasoning

8

Strategies for Metacognition

When students reflect on *how* they learn, they become better learners. This is metacognition—being aware of how we think. Research on expertise also suggests that when individuals are aware of their own thinking processes, they can regulate their thoughts and actions to maximize learning and performance. Experts are aware of what they don't know but need to know, whereas novices lack this awareness. Developing metacognition helps learners uncover the awareness of what they don't know so they can move forward to ask important questions. Basically, when we are *aware* of what we think and do we can *manage* what we think and do. This chapter focuses on the "Metacognition" Stretch Prompt (see Figure 8.1).

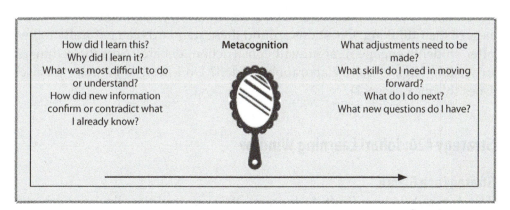

How did I learn this?
Why did I learn it?
What was most difficult to do
or understand?
How did new information
confirm or contradict what
I already know?

Metacognition

What adjustments need to be
made?
What skills do I need in moving
forward?
What do I do next?
What new questions do I have?

Figure 8.1 Metacognition Stretch Prompt

On Tests ↑ Help Me gather info

DOI: 10.4324/9781003293286-9

What I did to complete Book Study.

When considering talent development, metacognitive skills not only enhance self-awareness of personal strengths but also pave the way for navigating potential challenges or setbacks that come with pursuing long-term goals. When students use metacognition, it provides the link between a future goal and the current reality by allowing the learner to explicitly think through the steps to take to meet a goal.

This chapter describes strategies for metacognition to guide students to be self-aware of their own thinking and approaches in learning. In applying metacognition, students can reflect on next steps to learn new information, apply problem solving, and improve performance. As such, these reflections are key to strategic thinking. In this chapter, I also include meta-affective strategies, those that promote awareness of regulating emotion in the process of learning. When students encounter setbacks or challenges, they might experience frustration, fear, stress, self-doubt, or anxiety. Becoming aware of emotion allows individuals to manage emotion and move forward with resilience. *★Mars Span! ★*

You can enhance metacognition by prompting students to regularly think about how they plan, monitor, and evaluate their learning. This can be ongoing through instruction and does not necessarily need to be addressed as a separate "activity" in designing a lesson. These strategies work well when integrated into self-assessments, exit tickets, or as prompts to start a lesson or goal. The key idea is to guide students to reflect on "how" they analyzed content, how they generated new ideas, how they became aware of misconceptions, how they discovered connections, how they applied critical thinking, and how they worked around obstacles. These "how" reflections build agency as students link their effort and actions to outcomes.

As mentioned previously in Chapter 2, students can reflect on their own thinking and reasoning using the prompts for Paul and Elder's (2019) Intellectual Standards. These can be used for students to reflect on the clarity, accuracy, relevance, precision, depth, breadth, logic, significance, and fairness of their thinking. Questions around these standards can naturally follow after students engage in argument construction, debates, Socratic seminars, or writing (e.g., Is more elaboration needed? Do I need to be more precise? Does this make sense?).

Strategy #20: Johari Learning Window

Strategy at a Glance

The Johari Window (Luft & Ingram, 1955) is traditionally used to gain self-awareness and enhance interpersonal relationships. In the open window a person reveals a quality, adjective, or personal characteristic that others already know (e.g., I am good at playing basketball; most people see me as helpful, and I agree). In the blind spot window, an individual learns more self-awareness when attending to feedback (positive or negative) given by another person (e.g., sometimes you interrupt others when you talk; you are really good at creative illustrations!) The hidden spot includes things the individual knows but others do not know (e.g., my feelings were hurt when I was not invited to the party). The unknown window is "untapped"; that is, these are aspects of an individual that are not known to self or to others because an opportunity has not been presented to reveal these qualities. For example, who will you be in ten years? What would happen if you continued to practice ___, every day? How might your talents grow? As more aspects of each window are revealed, the "open" window gets larger, and so, the interpersonal relationships are enhanced while the individual continues to gain self-awareness (see Figure 8.2). This traditional model is useful in building a sense of community and belongingness within a classroom as students share about themselves and as they point out strengths they see each other.

This strategy can be adapted to enhance awareness of how *learning* about a topic changes over time and how pursuit of that learning might continue. In the open window, students can share what they already know about a given topic (this might occur as an introductory part of a lesson). Throughout the lesson or unit, students can revisit the window to uncover "blind spots" that were revealed with interactions with peers, resources, or interactions with the teacher. Here students can reflect on how they came to understand the content more clearly and be reflective of preconceptions or biased judgments they had about the content before deeper study. In the hidden window, students have an opportunity to reflect on their strengths in learning by reflecting on areas they feel confident they can teach others. In the unknown window, students reflect on what is still "unknown" even after pursuing this topic in-depth. Here they reflect on new questions and curiosities that result from the learning. As shown in Figure 8.3, reflections in the Johari Learning

	Known to Me	Not Known to Me
Known to Others	Open	Blind
Not Known to Others	Hidden	Unknown

Figure 8.2 Traditional Johari Window (Self-Awareness)

Source: The Johari window was developed by Luft and Ingram (1955).

	Known to Me	Not Known to Me
Known to Others	Open *What I already knew about the topic*	Blind *I did not realize_____, before, but ____ has helped me understand it more clearly.* *I realize now I had a preconceived notion of___.* *____* *I am now more self-aware of a bias in my reasoning-* *I used to think, now I realize___ because___.*
Not Known to Others	Hidden *Something I know about this topic that I can teach others*	Unknown *I still know I don't know__,* *but I would like to know more about___.* *I am still wondering about__.*

Figure 8.3 Johari Learning Window for Reflection

Source: Adapted from Original Johari Window by Luft and Ingram (1955). Redraw, *wants first* column text turns sideways

Window open doors for new inquiry (unknown), allow students to see how their learning was impacted (open window and blind spot), and how they might contribute to the learning of others (hidden window).

Strategy #21: The Ripple Reflection

Strategy at a Glance

The Ripple Reflection allows students to reflect on past or current learning, responding to "What did I learn? How did I learn it? Why did I learn it? Now that I know___, what are my next steps?" (See Figure 8.4). By reflecting on what they learned, there is a ripple effect in how this learning affects their next steps. This might include new questions, insight on action they can take as a result of the learning, or how they might share their information with others. This type of reflection provides opportunities for students to monitor their thinking and emphasizes possibilities for new inquiry, all important skills critical to "thinking as an expert."

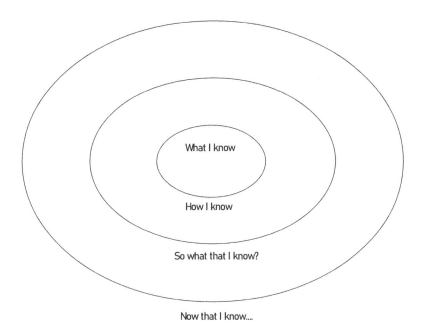

Figure 8.4 Ripple Reflection

Alternatively, this can be used as students plan ahead on a task. They can start with their articulated motivation (why) and link this to what they will learn through the mid-link of "how" they will learn it: "Why will learn it, What will I do/learn, and How will I do/learn it?" Reflecting on the reason for learning and actions taken in learning builds agency because students can make the direct connection between their action (how they learn) and the outcome (the learning), tied to a motivation for doing so (why they learned).

Ask students to continue to think about the thought process beyond the "how." Students can develop their own "how" questions, or you may suggest some of the following. Students may enjoy making their thinking visible through sketching these ideas or elaborating in group discussions.

1. How did you generate ideas?
2. How did you determine best ideas?
3. How did you think of ways to elaborate on ideas?
4. How did you change in this process?
5. How did the steps lead to original innovation?
6. How did you determine bias?
7. How did you make decisions?
8. How did you become aware of your misconceptions?

Reflection Prompts	Response
• What I know:_____ (Major facts, concepts, relationships that I learned)	
• How I know:_____ (What I did to learn this)	
• So what that I know:_____ (This will help me____ This makes me realize_____)	
• Now that I know, _____ (Next steps, new questions, adjustments)	

Figure 8.5 Ripple Reflection Prompts

Beyond using the circle as a visual, you could include the following prompts for end of lesson exit tickets or reflections as part of self-assessments. Example prompts are shown in Figure 8.5.

On a related note, Hattie's work on visible learning (Hattie, 2012) suggests the power of teacher clarity in affecting student learning when students can answer these questions—What am I learning? Why am I learning it? How will I know when I have learned it? Providing related reflection prompts that ripple into "next steps" for learning provide opportunities for future inquiry.

Strategy #22: Mind Maps

Strategy at a Glance
Mind maps are visual hierarchical maps that show how ideas and concepts are related to one another. Though there are a number of different variants, the term "mindmapping" is officially trademarked by Tony Buzan (Buzan & Buzan, 1993) as a strategy to organize ideas, comprehend ideas, and create new ideas. It facilitates thinking about any concept or topic with additions of associations, images, and words branching from the main concept. These are useful as students take notes, brainstorm ideas, or make their thinking visible to show how they understand a complex concept. Mind maps help us "see" what students are thinking, giving us insight to knowing how students understand the interrelationships between ideas, where they might have misconceptions, and how we might extend their learning.

How is mind-mapping a metacognitive strategy? To be honest, I have written this strategy in and out of various chapters in this text. It jogs creative thinking by promoting fluency and elaboration of ideas, enhances problem solving by illuminating the effects of a problem or issue, develops analytical thinking by showing complexities or perspectives of issues, and provides a thinking map for researching information from multiple sources. However, at its core, mind maps make thinking visible by illustrating the relationships between ideas; thus, mind maps help learners think about their own thinking (metacognition). Further, thinking maps can be used for strategic thinking (e.g., reasoning through an issue or developing a solution) or even planning for taking steps to complete a project. The inclusion of color, hierarchies, and images help clarify thinking about ideas and concepts. As students write ideas on smaller branches, sprouting off from the larger branches, they can dive into a deeper exploration of a topic beyond the surface level.

Mind maps are typically made with the following features (Buzan & Buzan, 1993):

1. Use blank paper with landscape orientation.
2. The central idea should be in the middle of the paper, shown as a visual image.
3. Make first level branches of associations stemming from the central idea. These should be on curved rather than straight lines. Add new branches of associations, up to 7 levels. Each level allows for greater depth of exploration.
4. The associations should be written as key words (not long phrases).
5. Add images and other visual elements to the mind map (which can sometimes convey more information than a word).
6. Use color intentionally on the mind map (e.g., color branches different colors) as this is important to remembering the content or evoking imagination with the content.

Example: Mind Map Applied to Managing Stress

In this example, a mind map prompt is used to guide a student's thinking around a specific stressor or issue (e.g., overwhelmed with a large project, did not win a competition). The mind map serves as a metacognitive tool for examining one's thoughts about the stressor. Worry can consume one's thoughts, and sometimes it is helpful to simply reflect on the stressor or worry to unravel meaning and decide on action to take. In this example, a student might identify a stressor with branches related to their emotions, purposes of the emotions, and possible steps to address the problem. Being able to be

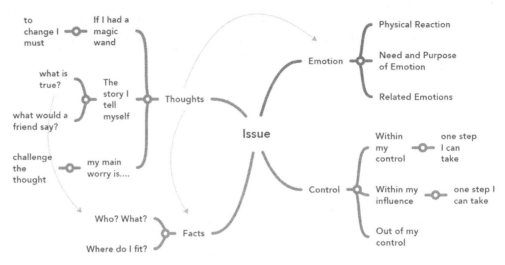

Figure 8.6 Mind Map for Thinking Through Stress/Issue

aware of emotion is the first step to managing emotion. Thinking through various plans and options can alleviate anxiety as it creates a sense of control (Mofield & Parker Peters, 2018).

Other Ideas and Tips

◆ Mind maps can be easily used with other strategies. For example, as students think through an issue, they can add to the mind map by thinking through the Elements of Thought, Six Thinking Hats, or Cascade of Consequences.

◆ Students might apply creative thinking strategies (e.g., SCAMPER, Synectic Trigger Mechanisms) to continue to add and brainstorm ideas.

◆ Mind maps can be used to plan ideas and steps for long-term projects (including time management, resources, and specific tasks to complete).

◆ Students can revisit their mind maps throughout a unit of study (or lesson) to add newly learned content and connections.

Strategy #23: Reflecting on Relevance

Strategy at a Glance

Students should also have opportunities to reflect on the relevance of learning on their own lives. Deep learning ignites motivation and invites students to answer, "Why should I do this or learn this?" The answer to this question is "task value." Task value is an important factor of student motivation (Wigfield & Eccles, 1992) and can include intrinsic value (the enjoyment from the task), attainment value (the importance of doing well on a task because it is important to the student's identity), utility value (how important the task is for the student's future goals), and also cost (what's worth giving up for the effort required to perform the task). Studies have shown links between task value and student achievement (Durik et al., 2015; Wigfield & Eccles, 2000).

When students are offered a variety of choices in the how they learn (e.g., learning activities) and what they produce (e.g., student products), and when students are also afforded opportunities to provide their own input into their learning based on their interests, this can greatly enhance task value. To specifically address utility value, studies have shown that written reflections on how and why the content is relevant can greatly affect motivation in challenging courses. Here, I have adapted an intervention described by Harackiewicz et al. (2016) used among university students to apply to K-12 students:
Relevance Reflection Prompt:

> In a brief writing response, mind-mapping activity, or sketch, explain the relevance of the lesson to your own life. Include concrete information from what you just learned. Explain or show how this information is relevant to you or useful to you. Explain or show how the learning applies to you and give examples. (Adapted from Harackiewicz et al., 2016, p. 749)

Giving opportunities for students to reflect on relevance cannot be overlooked. This metacognitive strategy allows students to "think about their thinking" in future contexts, enhancing a powerful motivational lever in knowing why the learning matters.

Strategy #24: WOOP—A Goal Attainment Strategy

Strategy At a Glance
WOOP—an acronym for wish, outcome, obstacle, plan—is a strategy used to drive motivation in reaching self-set personal goals. In psychology, it is known as *mental contrasting with implementation intentions* (MC-II; Oettingen & Gollwitzer, 2010). The four-step process evokes positive feelings when an individual considers an important goal (wish) and

envisions positive outcomes associated with reaching this goal (outcome). Then, obstacles are considered which evoke a negative feeling, igniting a cognitive "angst" to get past the obstacle. This "contrast" creates a motivation for an individual to make a plan in order to move beyond the obstacle should it occur. From here, the individual creates a plan as an if-then statement that can be used to navigate the obstacle and, therefore, achieve the important goal that was set. Though SMART goals are often popular among educators and students, they do not include the opportunities to pre-plan strategies for managing obstacles. When an obstacle is made concrete (as in WOOP), a plan can be followed to manage the obstacle. This enhances resilience and tenacity for moving forward towards the goal.

The steps for WOOP include the following:

- ◆ Wish: Think of a goal you want to achieve that is meaningful and realistic to achieve.
- ◆ Outcome: Imagine the positive outcomes and positive emotions associated with achieving the goal.
- ◆ Obstacle: Ask, "What obstacles stand in your way of reaching your goals?" This might include time, fear, self-doubt, distractions, lack of motivation, lack of preparation, etc.
- ◆ Plan: Create an if-then plan to be followed if the obstacle occurs. This allows students to see the specific steps that allow them to make continual progress towards a goal.

Example: WOOP Applied to Creative Writing
In this example, a student uses WOOP to plan for a goal to be achieved within the next month.

- ◆ Wish: I want to submit my creative writing project to a competition.
- ◆ Outcome: I will feel a sense of accomplishment and pride for completing my work and sharing in a competition.
- ◆ Obstacle: The obstacle is that I do not like to polish my writing.
- ◆ Plan: If I feel a lack of motivation to edit and revise my writing, I will focus on one aspect at a time to revise, such as revising for character development.

Other Ideas and Tips

◆ Encourage students to visit their goals and plans established in WOOP throughout a given period of time and reflect on how they are making progress. Being aware of how progress is made as well as being aware of challenges that block progress empower students to make decisions, reflect on strengths and mistakes, and make plans for the next steps in their learning.

◆ Use WOOP for content-specific goals. This can bring awareness to specific skills that students want to develop within a content area (e.g., personal goal in writer's workshop).

◆ WOOP can be applied as a problem-solving strategy to think from the perspective of any real-life eminent individual or character in a novel or short story they are reading (e.g., What was a main goal for the individual? What obstacles did he or she have to overcome to achieve his or her goals? How might he or she think through WOOP? What might have been his or her wish, desired outcome, obstacle, and plan?)

◆ WOOP worksheets, an app, short video clips, and other guides are available at http://woopmylife.org.

Meta-affective Strategies

What can we do to integrate social-emotional learning into academic learning? Though some of this discussion is beyond the scope of this text, there are a number of strategies that can be incorporated into academic learning experiences, especially as reflection strategies. These are "meta-affective" strategies in that they bring awareness to students' affective (emotional) states. This is especially important in the context of cultivating psychosocial skills in talent development since emotions can catalyze or paralyze a student's motivation to continue through challenging pursuits (Mofield, 2020). Many of the strategies in Table 8.1 are adapted from previous work and research I have conducted with my colleague, Dr. Megan Parker Peters (see Mofield & Parker Peters, 2018 for more thorough explanations and lesson plans related to the strategies).

Table 8.1 Social-Emotional Learning Integration

Social-Emotional Concept	Strategies to be used through journaling, reflections, small-group discussion, exit tickets, etc.	Rationale
Self-Agency	What was the hardest part of the assignment? How did you get through it? How did you feel as you encountered the obstacle? How do you feel now? What were two "wins" you experienced today? What did you do to cause those "wins"?	Provides self-agency in understanding that personal action led to moving through the obstacle. Reinforces that effort led to success.
Perseverance	Reflect on the experiences of another character or individual (in Social Studies, Science, etc.). How did __persevere? How did ___ manage stress? What emotions did he/she experience? How did ___ understand and manage his/her emotions?	Allows for reflection of how others exhibit perseverance even with unpleasant emotions.
Problem Solving	Think of a challenge you are experiencing. Think of at least three ways you could approach this. Who may you seek out for support? What resources will you need?	Allows students to think through more than one way to solve a problem.
Time management	How can you break the task into smaller tasks? What timeline do you need to establish?	Strengthens self-regulation skills; provides a plan and a sense of control.

(Continued)

Table 8.1 (Continued)

Social-Emotional Concept	Strategies to be used through journaling, reflections, small-group discussion, exit tickets, etc.	Rationale
Explaining failure: learned optimism	Reinforce learned optimism: *It's this situation, this time, things can change, I will rise. Is this something I can control? If it is not, I will let go* Students may journal thinking through failure through the learned optimism lens.	Emphasizes belief that failure is not permanent, pervasive (in all contexts), or personal. This promotes the idea—some things you just can't control.
Interpersonal assertive communication: expressing need	Teach "I statements." "I feel___when____. Can we work toward. . . ?"	Teaches students a structure for assertive communication, allowing them to express frustration and needs to another person.
Handling criticism	Separate facts from feelings. Is this a pattern? What are you learning from this? What is your next step?	Allows for reflection of emotion and a plan for moving forward.
Goal-Setting for tenacity/ persistence	WOOP What is the <u>w</u>ish? (goal) What is the <u>o</u>utcome you hope for? What <u>o</u>bstacle might get in the way? What <u>p</u>lan will you have if you encounter the obstacle (if— then—)	Provides a plan for obstacles, motivating a student to persevere because there is a plan to follow.
Emotional awareness	Use an emotion wheel to identify the emotions of the main character throughout the story. Create a chart that shows how emotions correspond to experiences. (This can also apply personally to the student.)	Allows reflection for how others have experienced and managed emotion.

Social-Emotional Concept	Strategies to be used through journaling, reflections, small-group discussion, exit tickets, etc.	Rationale
Emotional awareness	Reflect on the purpose of the emotion you are experiencing (e.g., what does "anxiety" move or "tell" you to do? Why?).	Being aware of our emotions allows us to manage our emotions.
Interpersonal awareness	Think of a time you experienced a conflict, setback, challenge, or obstacle. What assumptions were made about the situation, and/or what stories did you tell yourself to explain the situation? How do emotions influence those assumptions or stories? How might you logically tackle those assumptions?	Teaches students that assumptions (stories we tell ourselves) are not always the reality. We have to be aware of our assumptions.
Stress/Anxiety	Reflect on whether the experienced stress is a threat or physical response to prepare you for an opportunity. Who might you reach out to for support? How can you break the task into smaller parts? What are other alternatives to solving the problem?	Students gain awareness for managing stress, anxiety, and other intense emotions.
Perfectionism	Guide students to be aware of self-talk and automatic negative thoughts. Help them reframe "I should" and "I must" thoughts into "It's okay if__ because___" thoughts. Ask students what's the worst possible outcome for not being perfect? What's the best possible outcome?	Reframing thoughts guides students to a healthy pursuit of excellence (rather than pursuit of perfection). Asking about best/worst case scenario helps students reason through the motivations of their perfectionism.

Source: Strategies adapted from Mofield and Parker Peters (2018) and Mofield (2020)

9

Planning for Deep Learning and Differentiation

In this chapter, I provide examples for planning for DOK Level 4 tasks (e.g., arrive at a large conclusion, justify conclusions from multiple resources, develop solutions for real-world problems, or apply/transfer their learning to multiple contexts and conditions). These tasks often take more than one class period to complete and involve multiple sources. This chapter focuses on the "Transfer" Stretch Prompt (see Figure 9.1) and synthesizes content from the previous chapters.

I also show how to use all the strategies and Stretch Prompts (see Chapter 2) to differentiate instruction. This includes modifying student tasks, products, and assessments to be more complex for individual students. These strategies

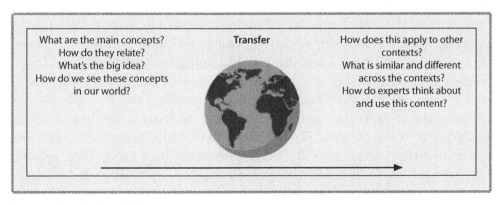

Figure 9.1 Transfer Stretch Prompt

DOI: 10.4324/9781003293286-10

can also be used within whole group instruction, with various levels of scaffolds added to support student learning. The chapter closes with a model for supporting students from culturally, linguistically, and economically diverse backgrounds and twice-exceptional students in accessing rigorous content.

Planning for Deep Learning

First things first. Don't skip the pre-assessment as part of instructional planning. A pre-assessment should be given to all students in order to glean insight into what students already know about content. Pre-assessments can be given in the form of concept maps, mind maps, one-page summaries, short tests, or more formal end-of-unit tests (given before the unit is taught). The pre-assessment should ideally allow you to see what students know, understand, and what they already do/think regarding the content. Be careful in relying solely on unit tests if they capture only knowledge goals. It is important to know the extent to which students understand the "so what" of the content (understand goals) as well as how students use reasoning to think about the content at higher levels (process/do goals).

Before deciding how to pre-assess, you must determine what to pre-assess by determining the learning goals of the lesson. As described in Chapter 2, take time to write knowledge goals based on *what* facts and information that students should learn, understanding goals based on an enduring idea from an essential question (*why* this learning endures), and process goals based on *how* students think about the content (e.g., analytical, creative, and critical thinking).

Once you have thoughtfully considered your learning goals, then you can develop a short pre-assessment to understand where students are in relation to these goals. The use of concept maps or mind maps can be especially useful because it helps you see how students organize their thinking through hierarchical structures, allowing you to know students' understanding about relationships between concepts. Understanding goals can be assessed by asking students to provide examples about big ideas based on their prior knowledge (e.g., provide an example from your own experience of how geography, climate, and natural resources affect people's lives). Process goals can be pre-assessed by asking students to apply reasoning, analysis, or thinking as a scientist/mathematician/historian to demonstrate how they "grapple with" and apply what they know (e.g., explain why Ancient Egypt flourished as a civilization). Sometimes gifted students have an extensive *knowledge* of a content area, but not necessarily deep *understanding* of the content. Therefore, you can differentiate by providing learning opportunities that emphasize the enduring understandings and high-level processing (and this happens by incorporating the strategies from the previous chapters).

From here, you can develop a lesson sequence with an aim for leading students to accomplish a DOK Level 4 task. You might want to use backwards planning by first thinking about the DOK Level 4 tasks before planning out a sequenced lesson. Consider, "what can students ultimately do with this information?" As a reminder from Chapter 1, DOK Level 4 tasks include the use of multiple resources and might involve multiple days to accomplish. These tasks require students to arrive at a large conclusion, restructure data, or develop a solution to a real-world issue. In the preparation part of the lesson sequence, consider how you will prepare students with pre-work before they directly engage in the complex task. In Engagement, plan for how students will interact and engage with the content to apply new learning, and in the Extension, consider how you might even extend learning further for additional depth or breadth. As you plan for each phase, think about how the strategies presented throughout this book fit to support students' conceptual, analytical, creative, or critical thinking.

In the examples in Tables 9.1–9.3 that follow, I provide examples of a "big picture" structure that might guide your planning process, though other specific parts of the lesson/unit (e.g., delivery of content, specific questions, assessment details) should be considered within a more detailed plan.

Table 9.1 Planning Elementary English Language Arts

Essential Question	Does conflict lead to opportunity or chaos?
Knowledge Goal	Students will know how characters develop within a story and know elements of plot
Understanding Goal (Enduring Understanding)	Students will understand *that* the conflict contributes to the development of character
Process (Do) Goal	Students will defend an argument, examine underlying motivations, and forecast long-term consequences of a character's decision.
DOK 4 Task	Does conflict lead to opportunity or to chaos? Use information from at least three fairy tales to defend an argument, noting how conflict contributed to the development of the character.

Preparing for the Task	To prepare to answer this question, students might complete a number of activities to explore the nature of conflict in the fairy tales. For example, students might conduct an Iceberg of Why's to determine the root cause of conflict in each story, then relate how this conflict affected the character. They might also create a Cascade of Consequences or Double Fishbone organizer to show multiple effects of the conflict in the story (including how this affected the character), or they might even conduct a POWER analysis on each story to determine how power and conflict relate.
Engagement	After exploring conflict in the preparation phase, students may then be prepared to develop a strong argument for "Does conflict lead to opportunity or chaos?" using the Argument Construction Model. Students present their work in a multimedia presentation that also generalizes the big idea "conflict leads to change" to real-life or other stories.
Extension	Students can continue to engage in creative thinking by re-creating a fable or fairy tale using any of the creative thinking strategies (e.g., SCAMPER, Synectic Trigger Mechanisms) to modify the conflict and show how it changed later outcomes and opportunities for the character.

Table 9.2 Planning Math Estimation

Essential Question	**How do we make reasonable estimates?**
Knowledge Goal	Students will use estimation and percentages to solve real-world problems.
Understanding Goal (Enduring Understanding)	Students will understand *that* estimation is useful for approximation though limited with precision.
Process (Do) Goal	Students will apply Elements of Thought (examine data, inferences, points of view, implications) to approach an estimation real-world problem.

(Continued)

Table 9.2 (Continued)

DOK 4 Task	What percent of a person's life is spent on "screen time?" Develop a plan to estimate your data and present your reasoning and conclusions to the class.
Preparing for the Task	Students think through a plan for collecting data, using The Ripple Reflection—Why am I learning this, how will I do this, what do I know?
Engagement	Students use Elements of Thought to support how they arrive at their conclusion. What *evidence* would they collect and how would they do so? What *inferences* would they make from this evidence? What points of view are considered? Why is this a relevant *issue*? What are the *implications* of their conclusions? What interferes with *accuracy, precision*, and *relevance* (see Intellectual Standards of Reasoning Ch. 2)?
Extension	Students use the Six Thinking Hats model to explore various perspectives of screen time. Students might also write an editorial after doing some additional research using an argument technique to express opinions about "how much" screen time is too much.

Table 9.3 Planning Social Studies

Essential Question	**Is sacrifice necessary for progress?**
Knowledge Goal	Students will know important people, ideas, and events of the women's suffrage movement.
Understanding Goal (Enduring Understanding)	Students will understand *that* societal change happens from multiple influences.
Process (Do) Goal	Students will examine patterns and make connections from past ideas to current ideas.
DOK 4 Task	What types of social movements throughout American history and today are similar to the Women's suffrage movement? Use multiple sources to create a presentation to depict patterns of social justice and how these are relevant to issues of today.

Preparing for the Task	To prepare, students collect data and facts from several sources. Students might start their investigations with questions they generate from the Wonder Window. To organize ideas, students might use portions of the Metapattern Map applied to the Suffrage movement and at least one other movement.
Engagement	Students will use Metaphorical Thinking (Extended Synectics) to list important facts and ideas from the Women's Suffrage movement to facts and ideas of another social movement. They will make matches across the columns to determine how the movements are similar.
Extension	Students use the "Random Input" (Forced Associations) strategy to brainstorm ideas for promoting awareness around a social issue of their own in a new, fresh, creative way.

Planning for Differentiated Tasks

How might we create tasks that are "bumped up" a notch to provide additional layers of complexity? The use of tiering is a common approach to adjusting tasks and assignments. I propose that by adjusting the task to include a "why" and/or "what if" strategy, the task allows for more complex levels of thought. This follows the same structure as the Know-Relate-Extend Model (see Figure 9.2).

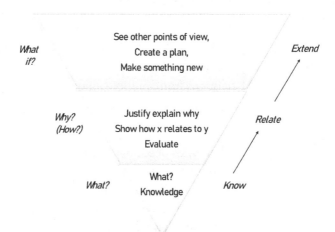

Figure 9.2 Know, Relate, Extend: What, Why, and What if Thinking

Table 9.4 organizes strategies and prompts by "Why" and "What if" thinking. As you create tiered assignments with more complexity, these thinking prompts can provide options for making adjustments to the process and/or product, thereby increasing cognitive demands of the task.

Table 9.4 Guide for Adding Vertical Differentiation to Tasks

Quick Reference		Strategies	Thinking Prompts
Why?/How? (Relate)	Justify, explain why	• Argument Construction Model • Iceberg of Why's • Balloon Debate	• Debate ____ • Should___? • What is the underlying issue and why? • Use Elements of Thought to justify___
	Show how x relates to y	• Connections Web • Schema Board • Inductive Reasoning • Synectic Analogies • Forced Associations • Metapatterns	• How do__,__, and ___ interrelate? • How does ___ contribute to__? • How does understanding this relationship provide new insight on __?
	Evaluate	• SWOT • Should-Could-Would criteria	• What criteria should be considered? • Which is better? Why?
What if? (Extend)	See Points of View	• Six Thinking Hats • POWER Analysis • Argument Construction Models • Synectic Analogies	• What are the assumptions and implications of these points of view? • What if these points of view were considered? • How is ___ like___and how is it not like__?
	Create a plan or something new	• SCAMPER Stretch • Synectic Triggers • Cascade of Consequences	• How might you modify__ to improve___? • What are the short and long-term consequences of___? • What if this is applied in other contexts? • What would happen if…?

In the Table 9.5, you can see how a typical task is made more complex by adding a dimension for "why" and further by adding a feature from "what if"? In tiering for challenge, process, and product, the leveled tasks allow for students to learn according to their readiness. This provides students opportunities to build their understanding if they need continued reinforcement of

Table 9.5 Tiering Assignments with Why and What if?

Tier 1-Know	Tier 2- Relate	Tier 3- Relate + Extend
Create a brochure about landforms, highlighting the key features of each.	Create a brochure about landforms. Explain the effects the landform has on the living things that live there.	Create a model that shows how climate affects this landform and how landforms affect weather patterns. Should humans interfere with changing landforms? Why or why not? Explain what happens when humans interfere on a given landform (e.g., deltas).
Complete the graphic organizer to show the sequence of events of the plot. Use evidence from the text to support your response.	Complete an Iceberg of Why's for an important plot event in the story to show the influence of other plot events and character actions.	What major decisions does the plot event cause the character to consider? Use the Should-Could-Would criteria and apply it to the character. Create a Cascade of Consequences for the possible new outcomes of the story based on possible decisions.
Develop a creative presentation or product to show the most important contributions of FDR (e.g., write a song, present a monologue, make a game).	Develop a creative presentation or product to show and justify the most important contributions of FDR. Use the Metapatterns Map to guide your thinking and explain how at least four Metapatterns are evident in his contributions.	Develop a creative presentation or product to show and justify the most important contributions of FDR. Explain how others might have viewed his initiatives (using Six Thinking Hats) and suggest a way for one of his contributions to be tweaked for current times (use SCAMPER).

(Continued)

Table 9.5 (Continued)

Tier 1-Know	Tier 2- Relate	Tier 3- Relate + Extend
Estimate how many watts of energy your home uses in a month.	Estimate how many watts of energy your home uses in a month. Determine what should be "cut" to decrease watts used by 20%? (Use Should-Could-Would criteria).	Estimate how many watts of energy your home uses in a month. Determine what should be cut to decrease watts used by 20%. Create a defensible plan using the Argument Construction Model.

the learning (Tier level 1) or provides opportunities to extend their learning (Tier level 2 and 3).

It is important to tactfully present tiered assignments to students. This involves using flexible grouping (where students are not always locked into a tier) over time based on pre-assessment data. You can also work to make tiering invisible by using various colors of paper, stickers, or numbers for groups of students in various levels. If tiering is used regularly, then students are more likely to understand that flexible assignments and grouping are part of the culture and climate of the classroom environment. Another option is for students to self-select the tier and provide a reason for why they will be challenged at that level. Overall, tiering can be an effective way to vary the level of tasks while supporting and challenging all students.

Strategy #25: "Show You Know" Board

In efforts to provide students with opportunities to choose tasks according to their interests, students are often provided options from choice boards and menus. There are many resources available, especially in gifted education, which provide examples of choice boards for various grade levels and content areas. However, sometimes the focus of the choice board is on the type of products students make rather than the type of thinking used to make the product. It is important to consider the level of cognitive demand required in many of the choice boards. Consider the following questions:

◆ Does the task allow students to engage in higher levels of analysis?
◆ Does the task allow for students to apply strategic reasoning?

◆ Does the task allow students to make insightful connections?
◆ Does the task lead to deeper learning?

Sometimes these choice boards simply need slight adjustments. You may use the Stretch Prompts (see Chapter 2 or refer to Resource 9.2) to increase the challenge level of the tasks on choice boards. While I do believe choice is a powerful motivator for students, providing 3–5 choices is often enough. I have noticed from working with teachers over the years in various school districts, it can become quite burdensome to think of 9 options on a 3 x 3 choice board or create elaborate "menus" with various point levels for different types of tasks. This often overcomplicates differentiation.

One approach for developing choice is to use the Show You Know Board as shown in Resource 9.1. This tool can be used as a planning guide as teachers create at least three product options for students. Each option is representative of critical/analytical thinking, creative thinking, and contextual thinking, loosely based on Sternberg's types of intelligence (Sternberg, 1997). This board allows for all students to answer the same essential question through various product choices. Students must demonstrate the answer to the essential question within their product whether it be a digital poster, an interview, model, or other form.

Teachers can discern what types of products are most appropriate for a content area and age group. I do like to emphasize that students should be given opportunities to make authentic products representative of what disciplinarians actually do (e.g., design a model in science), though students also enjoy being creative in sharing their learning products that are related to their interests (e.g., creating songs, creative visuals). This planning guide builds in opportunities for students to demonstrate what they understand about the concepts by answering the essential question and uses prompts that elicit creative, critical, and contextual thinking. In this way, the focus is not so much about the type of product but about the type of thinking a student uses to produce the product.

As shown in Table 9.6 and 9.7, a choice menu can be created to show three options for students, each representing one type of activity from the Show You Know Planning Board. Alternatively, this board can be used to plan creative activities for students at learning stations or applied to other assignments. You may create your own three-choice menu using the editable document for Resource 7.1 at www.routledge.com/9781032275581.

Show you know
Essential Question
How can___ be applied to___? How does___ influence___?
Why does__? How is__?
What is the purpose of___ in___? Should____ or____?
What is happening and why?

Make/Design/Create___		
Poster (digital)	Infographic	Model
Advertisement	Presentation	Conversation between__
Letter	Interview with__	and__.
Song/Poem	Lesson	Monologue
Visual	Newspaper article	Your own graphic organizer
Plan	Proposal	Written response (short essay)
		Invention/Solution

Critical/Analytical Thinking	**Creative Thinking**	**Contextual Thinking**
• Show how ___, ___ and ____ relate to/causes ____. What if__changed? Show examples of these relationships. • Show an argument for/against___. Include reasons, evidence, and implications. • Show an argument for/against. Defend your argument explaining how concepts interact. • Show the decision that needs to be made and criteria used to make a decision. (Consider feasibility and impact.) • Show a prediction/hypothesis based on the relationships you see between ___, ___, and ___.	• Show how to improve___ so that___. • Show a new way to ___ and how this would benefit___. • Show how ____ is like___ (at least 5 ways). • Show a plan for solving____, considering multiple effects of the solution. • Show how___ would see the situation/issue. What are their underlying assumptions, values, thoughts, questions?	• Show how this works in a real-world situation and how it can be used in the future. • Show many examples of how the big idea_____ relates to this content. Then show how the big idea____ also works in other contexts. • Show how if____ were applied to another context, what would be the same and what would be different? • Show a plan for solving____ explaining how the problem is similar to another situation or context.

Be sure to answer the Essential Question in your response.

Resource 9.1 Show You Know Planning Board

Table 9.6 Show You Know Board: Student Chooses One of Three Options—Science

Essential Question How is the earth, sun, and moon a system? Choose one:		
Critical Thinking	**Creative Thinking**	**Contextual Thinking**
Make a model to show the relationships between the Earth, sun and moon and how they operate as a system. What criteria should be established to determine it is a system? Be sure to include a written response to the essential question.	Make an interview with a meteorologist to show how he/she views the Earth, sun, and moon as a system. What assumptions, thoughts, and questions do meteorologists consider through the interactions of the earth, sun, and moon in a system? Be sure to answer the essential question in your response.	Make a conversation between the Earth and Mars to explain what would be the same and what would be different about the systems between the planet, moons, and sun. Be sure to answer the essential question within the conversation.

Table 9.7 Show You Know Board: Student Chooses One of Three Options—English Language Arts

Essential Question What motivates a character? Choose one:		
Critical Thinking	**Creative Thinking**	**Contextual Thinking**
Perform a monologue to show how change, power, and needs affect the character's motivation. How does the character's problem affect their motivation? Be sure to answer the essential question in your response.	Conduct an interview with the main character in the book. In the interview, show how the character wished to improve the situation he was in so that he could accomplish his own goals. Be sure to answer the essential question in your interview.	Make a graphic organizer to show many examples of how the big idea "change can be positive or negative" relates to the character's motivation. Then explain how this idea "change can be positive or negative" is also relevant in other stories. Be sure to answer the essential question.

Assessing for Understanding

How do you assess for deep learning? Whether in the form of formative or summative assessments, you can use criteria from the critical and creative thinking taxonomies (in Chapter 2) and other models (e.g., Paul's Elements of Thought and Intellectual Standards, DOK Level criteria) for assessment. Consider what would it look like and sound like when students are learning for deeper understanding? The criteria in Figure 9.3 can serve as quick "look-fors" in student work and discussion as they engage in learning activities and various assessments.

When expecting students to show what they know on differentiated tasks, you also need a plan for differentiated assessments. Figure 9.4 shows an example of a rubric for the Show You Know Board. The product criteria assess students' understanding of content as applied to answering the essential question. Then, depending on whether a student chose the creative, critical, or contextual option, that specific feature of the rubric would also be applied to assess student understanding. This rubric allows you to make sure you are assessing *thinking*, not just completion and appearance criteria. Note that the rubric can be adapted by adding or taking away specific criteria, depending on what students are expected to demonstrate in their learning.

Students are using critical thinking by
- Examining missing parts
- Making judgments
- Question arguments
- Judging credibility and evidence
- Looking at other points of view
- Examining how parts work together as a whole
- Making cause-effect statements
- Explaining effects of effects
- Discussing interactions between elements
- Explaining contributions of x on y

Students are using creative thinking by
- Developing alternative solutions
- Making connections between two seemingly unrelated things
- Redesigning or rearranging for a specific purpose
- Developing a new approach or plan

Figure 9.3 Student Behaviors: Critical and Creative Thinking

	4 - Exceeds Expectations	3 - Meets Expectations	2 - Approaches Expectations and needs effort	1 - Needs Effort
Product	High-quality product answers the essential question insightfully. Demonstrates application of advanced vocabulary, language of the discipline, and accurate portrayal of newly learned content.	High-quality product answers the essential question and demonstrates learning related to the content area. Demonstrates application of grade-level vocabulary, language of the discipline, and accurate portrayal of newly learned content.	Product demonstrates learning related to the content area. Demonstrates some application of grade-level vocabulary, language of the discipline, and portrayal of newly learned content, though some elements may be missing.	Product lacks detail and/or does not adequately reflect content learning. Does not demonstrate adequate application of grade-level vocabulary, language of the discipline, and portrayal of newly learned content.
Critical Thinking	Demonstrates substantial evidence of logical reasoning through analysis, argument construction, well-supported predictions, and/or criteria development for decision-making.	Demonstrates some evidence of logical reasoning through analysis, argument construction, predictions, and/or criteria for decision-making.	Demonstrates some analysis or logical reasoning, though there might be gaps in connections, argument construction, predictions, and development of criteria.	Little or no evidence of analytical or logical reasoning is shown within the product.
Creative Thinking	Shows substantive evidence of varied, elaborate, and/or original ideas applied to content.	Shows some evidence of many, varied, elaborate, and/or original ideas applied to content.	Shows little evidence of varied, elaborate, and/or original thinking applied to content.	Does not show evidence of creative thinking. Demonstrates only summary of facts.
Contextual Thinking	Makes insightful applications of content to other contexts and/or disciplines.	Makes some applications of content to other contexts.	Only loose connections are made to contexts beyond the content studied.	Little or no connections are made to other contexts.

Figure 9.4 Example Rubric for Show You Know Board

Source: Adapted from Mofield and Phelps (2020).

Scaffolds and Supports for Students from Diverse Backgrounds/Twice-Exceptional

Plan with Assets, Values, and Strengths

When planning vertical differentiation, it is important to consider how to provide scaffolds and supports for students from culturally, linguistically, and economically diverse (CLED) backgrounds to access and engage in rigorous curriculum and instruction. We must work to provide instruction that is culturally relevant and responsive to students and use students' funds of knowledge as entry points into a lesson. When discussing students from diverse backgrounds, we should recognize that not all students who are impacted from poverty are culturally diverse, not all students who are multilingual are necessarily students impacted by poverty. While there is overlap for some students, we should keep in mind that all instruction should be responsive to students' readiness levels and identities. In addition, twice-exceptional students may need additional scaffolding to access rigorous content. The ideas presented here also apply to addressing their unique learning needs, with a key consideration to engage students where they in order to support their learning.

In the model Figure 9.4, you will notice that the bridge to rigorous curriculum begins with considering students' strengths, assets, and values. This strength-based approach to pedagogy emphasizes the importance of valuing students' backgrounds and cultural experiences as assets that students bring to the classroom. Students bring funds of knowledge (skills, knowledge, and life experiences) that they have learned from their family and cultural communities. When integrated into the curriculum, these funds of knowledge can be used to create rich learning experiences for students. Teachers can plan curriculum with student assets when they invite students to share about their personal lives and culture or when efforts are made to visit families (or invite parents to be involved in lessons). For example, if a student's family lives on land used for farming a specific crop, the student might be knowledgeable about certain agricultural practices which can easily be connected to science and social studies content.

Planning with funds of knowledge is a strengths-based approach to support students from CLED backgrounds. A strengths-based approach also includes planning instruction around what students can do (as opposed to what they "can't" speak, "don't" have, or what students "lack"). Rather than operating from a mindset that students lack background knowledge, we should value the identities and lived experiences of students and intentionally capitalize on their strengths and cultural backgrounds.

For example, multilingual learners have enhanced understanding about the structure of language, enhanced executive control, and strengths in cognitive flexibility in problem solving. Additionally, students learning a new language naturally take more risks in learning because as they engage in conversations they are playing with a new language. They also show high levels of intrinsic motivation compared to other students and can pay attention for up to 20% longer than typical students (Matthews & Castellano, 2014).

To support student self-identities, culturally-responsive instruction should teach students to value their own cultural heritage as well as those of others (Ford, 2011; Gay, 2018). Culturally-responsive instruction includes incorporating curriculum materials that mirror students' own lives, experiences, and culture. Figure 9.5 also shows additional instructional scaffolds that bridge access to differentiated features of gifted curriculum (advanced content, advanced process/product, and concepts).

Supporting Schema and Academic Language

When we plan with student strengths and experiences, we can further develop and integrate new learning into student schemas. One way of doing so is through front-loading. Front-loading can be used to prepare students for success in advanced programs (Briggs et al., 2008) by including explicit teaching of critical and creative thinking skills, pre-teaching vocabulary, and providing additional exposure to content through videos, and additional resources. Connecting the "new to the known" is a key way to connect learning to prior knowledge. The metaphorical connection strategies in Chapter 6 (e.g., Synectic Analogies, Forced Associations, Extended Synectics) can be especially appropriate scaffolds for strengthening students' understanding of the content by connecting the familiar to the unfamiliar. In doing so, we can promote meaning-making by linking learning to students' own experiences. This builds context for the learner and strengthens understanding of abstract concepts through concrete representations.

Other instructional scaffolds include planning intentionally to develop academic language (e.g., explicitly teach and model vocabulary and key terms, plan for deliberate dialogue and discussion). Many of the strategies in this book can be used to intentionally build schema and academic language (e.g., Connections Web and Schema Board). Additionally, the use of graphic organizers (e.g., Argument Construction Models, Cascade of Consequences) are powerful tools for supporting understanding abstract concepts by making thinking visible and concrete through a visual representation.

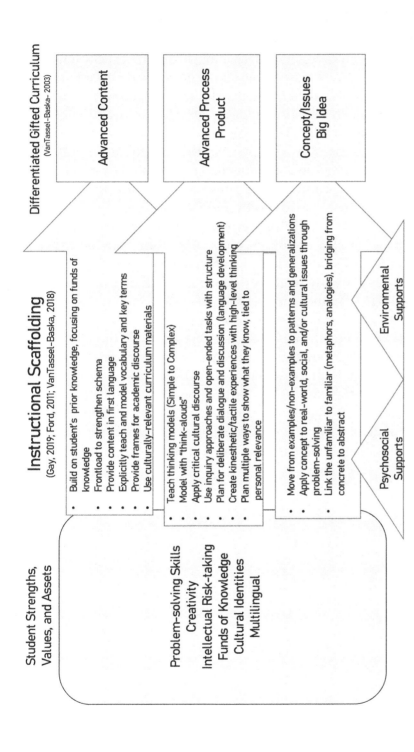

Figure 9.5 Bridging Access to Advanced Content

Source: Included in figure: (Gay, 2018; Ford, 2011; VanTassel-Baska, 2018; VanTassel-Baska & Baska, 2019)

This is an important consideration especially for twice-exceptional learners. Further, these models serve as structures for facilitating academic discourse within various content domains. They provide opportunities for students to use academic language in cause-effect reasoning, justifying conclusions, and examining relationships. When academic language is not practiced, it is not developed (Anderson, 2015); therefore, opportunities that allow for multiple verbal interactions through small-group discussions, debates, and think-pair share dialogue must be intentionally planned.

Academic language can also be supported through the use of sentence frames. Sentence frames provide a structure for supporting the production of high-level thinking responses so that students can spend less time thinking through how to phrase a response correctly and focus their cognitive effort on learning. These are often recommended supports for English language learners (ELLs), but they are also useful for supporting young students, twice-exceptional students, and students impacted by poverty.

The Stretch Prompts with sentence frames are included as a resource (See Resource 9.2). These frames provide a structure for student responses to high-level questions. Depending on the level of language proficiency, some students may need additional support such as a word bank, but as students progress in their learning, they may not need to rely on sentence frames. It is important to maintain high expectations for all students. When working with ELLs in particular, the World-Class Instruction, Design, and Assessment (WIDA Consortium, 2014) English Learning Development (ELD) standards can be useful in understanding the students' language proficiency and provides guidance on making strategic decisions on planning supports for ELLs across varying proficiency levels.

Stretch Prompts

Analysis

What are the parts of ___?
What is the overall structure?
How do parts relate to one another?

_____ is made up of the smaller parts such as_____
_____changes the structure.
_____ influences _____
_____relates to _____
_____changes_____

What happens if a part is removed?
What generalization can we make based on how the parts interact?

If _____is removed, then _____.
When ___ changes, we see its effect on_____.
The big idea is _____.

Problem Solving

What are the causes and effects of the problem/issue? What might happen if___?

_____, _____, and _____ cause the problem.
The effects of the problem are_____, _____, and _____.

What are the causes of the causes?
What are the effects of the effects?
What are unintended effects?
What do we not know about the problem? What do we need to know in order to make a plan?

___ caused the cause.
_____ is an effect of this effect.
We still need to know_____.

Creative Thinking for Solutions

What would need to be substituted, combined, adapted, modified, put to another use, eliminated, or rearranged to create a solution for ___ or improve ____?

This could be improved by_____.
We could try_____.

How have other problems like this been solved?
How might the idea/solution work in other contexts for other issues or problems?

When _____ happened, a solution was to___.
We could use this idea_____.
This can also work for_____.

Critical Thinking

What decisions need to be made about___?

We need to decide if___
Who___? What___?
When___? How___?

What criteria can we use to make our decision? How can we make fair, logical decisions?

Is it_____?
To what extent does it__?
What impact will ___ have on___?
We know we accomplish the goal when___.

SUPPORT MATERIAL

	Metaphorical Thinking	
How is ___ like ___? **Explain at least three ways** ___ is like ___ because Reason 1 _____ Reason 2 _____ Reason 3 _____		**How is ___ not like ___?** **What new metaphor can you make?** _____ is not like _____ because ___. _____ is like _____ because ___.

	Argument	
What is the debatable issue? **What are various perspectives?** **What evidence supports these perspectives?** Should _____? Is _____ or _____ better? _____ would think _____ because _____. ___ supports the idea _____.		**How can the claim be supported by the known relationship of concepts?** **What would strengthen the claim?** **Are claims fair, logical, accurate, and supported with evidence?** _____ is true because _____ interacts/causes _____. We could improve this claim by ___. The argument does not ___. The argument is strong because ___.

	Metacognition	
How did I learn this? Why did I learn it? **What was most difficult to do or understand?** **How did new information confirm or contradict what I already know?** I was successful by _____. This was important because _____. The most difficult part was _____. I already knew ___. I used to think ___ now I know ___.		**What adjustments need to be made?** **What skills do I need in moving forward?** **What do I do next?** **What new questions do I have?** I still need _____. Next, I will _____. I still wonder about _____.

	Transfer	
What are the main concepts? **How do they relate?** **What's the big idea?** **How do we see these concepts in our world?** The main concepts are ___, ___, and ___. ___ causes ___. ___ relates to ___. We see this big idea ___.		**How does this apply to other contexts?** **What is similar and different across the contexts?** **How do experts think about and use this content?** In this context we see _____, but in this context _____. An expert might ask _____. An expert may use this to _____.

Resource 9.2 Stretch Prompts with Frames

Belongingness and Mattering

As a teacher in the classroom, we are responsible for every students' belongingness and opportunity in that shared space, no matter their cultural background, socioeconomic status, or their home experiences. Beyond providing challenging instruction, good teaching involves affirming their identities and valuing who they are through psychosocial supports and environmental supports. Developing a sense of "belongingness" and "mattering" is essential for student success, therefore, we must convey that their thoughts, ideas, and opinions matter to the classroom community. We promote the idea of "intellectual mattering" (Schwartz, 2019) when we set protocols in our classrooms for conveying the value of student ideas. For example, we can teach students structures for peer-to-peer dialogue such as "Jade helped me understand the concept of__ better__when she shared___."

Likewise, as teachers, we can hold high expectations for students through the feedback we provide by using "wise feedback." Cohen et al. (1999) explain that this type of feedback conveys faith in their potential (I know you can do this) while being honest about the gap in reaching a learning goal (this is where you need to be, this is where you are). The key is to convey personal assurance that the student is capable and can improve. From here, you can provide specific actionable steps in writing and together track progress. On a similar note, it is important to explicitly teach students metacognitive strategies related to how to set goals, monitor progress towards these goals, create plans for obstacles, and promote the belief that ability grows from effort (see Chapter 8).

Concluding Thoughts

As educators, we are preparing students to apply their learning to an unknown future. Schools should be places where students engage in "real learning"—learning that matters to their own lives. Senge (1990) notes

> Real learning gets to the heart of what it means to be human. Through learning we re-create ourselves. Through learning we become able to do something we were never able to do. Through learning we reperceive our world and our connection to it.
>
> (pp. 13–14)

By planning instruction that requires students to strategically reason, make decisions, and problem solve through complex issues, we can stimulate, motivate, and challenge students while uncovering creative strengths and cultivating their talents. It is my hope that these strategies can help you teach students to move past a superficial understanding of facts towards a deep conceptual understanding of content. May these approaches inspire students to partake in *real* learning by asking new questions, making insightful connections, and imagining unknown possibilities. In doing so, students can know, show, and grow their budding strengths and gifts. Such learning sets the foundation for opportunity, innovation, and the flourishing development of potential and talent.

Appendix

Further Readings: Research/Theory to Practice

This appendix highlights a list of studies or conceptual/theoretical frameworks that support the use of various models described throughout this resource.

Schema Mental Models

- Brewer, W. F. (2000). Bartlett's concept of the schema and its impact on theories of knowledge representation in contemporary cognitive psychology. In A. Saito (Ed.), *Bartlett, culture and cognition* (pp. 69–89). Psychology Press.
- Lekshmi, D. (2020). Schema mental models and learning: An overview. *Journal of Critical Reviews*, 7(15), 2800–2807. https://doi.10.31838/jcr.07.15.382
- Weinstein, Y., Madan, C., & Sumeracki, M. (2018). Teaching the science of learning. *Cognitive Research: Principles and Implications*, 3(2), 1–17. https://doi.org/10.1186/s41235-017-0087-y

Student-Generated Questions

- Chiny, C. (2002). *Student-generated questions: Encouraging inquisitive minds in learning science.* https://repository.nie.edu.sg/handle/10497/292
- Luxton-Reilly, A., Denny, P., Plimmer, B., & Sheehan, R. (2012). *Activities and attitude: How student-generated questions assist learning. ITiCSE'12: Proceedings of the 17th ACM annual conference on Innovation and technology in computer science education.* https://doi.org/10.1145/2325296.2325302

Inductive Thinking Model

- Prusty, A. (2015). Effectiveness of inductive thinking model of teaching on history learning. *Pedagogy of Learning*, 1(1), 9–16.

◆ Taba, H. (1966). *Teaching strategies and cognitive functioning in Elementary School children (Cooperative Research Project)*. San Francisco State College.

Problem Finding and Creative Problem Solving

◆ Rubenstein, L. D., Callan, G. L., Shively, K., & Speirs Neumeister, K. (2021). The case of the hungry hippos: Supporting students' development of problem-finding strategies. *Gifted Child Today*, *44*(3), 128–140. https://doi.org/10.1177/10762175211008524
◆ Scott, G., Lentz, L. E., & Mumford, M. D. (2004). Types of creativity training. Approaches and their effectiveness. *Journal of Creative Behavior*, *38*(3), 149–179. https://doi.org/10.1002/j.2162-6057.2004.tb01238.x

Causal Analysis (Iceberg of Why's and Cascade of Consequences)

The strategies support students in second-order thinking (effects of effects) and examining the root of a problem before solving it.

◆ Byrne, C. L., Shipman, A. S., & Mumford, M. D. (2010). The effects of forecasting on creative problem-solving: An experimental study. *Creativity Research Journal*, *22*(2), 119–138. https://doi.org/10.1080/10400419.2010.481482.
◆ Hester, K. S., Robledo, I. S., Barrett, J. D., Peterson, D. R., Hougen, D. P., Day, E. A., & Mumford, M. D. (2012). Causal analysis to enhance creative problem-solving: Performance and effects on mental models. *Creativity Research Journal*, *24*, 115–133. https://doi.org/10.1080/10400419.2010.481482
◆ Moaveni, S., & Chou, K. C. (2016). Using the five whys method in the classroom: How to turn students into problem solvers. *Journal of STEM Education*, *17*(4), 35–41. www.jstem.org/index.php?journal=JSTEM&page=article&op=view&path%5B%5D=2171&path%5B%5D=1817

Six Thinking Hats

◆ Kivunja, C. (2015). Using De Bono's Six Thinking Hats Model to teach critical thinking and problem solving skills essential for success in the 21st Century Economy. *Creative Education, 6*(03), 380–391. https://doi:10.4236/ce.2015.63037

◆ Link, L. J., Wolberg, R. I., & Salmon, A. (2012). Creating a culture of thinking that cultivates the perspective-taking disposition. *A paper presented at South Florida Education Research Conference.* www.researchgate.net/publication/292488868_Creating_a_Culture_of_Thinking_that_Cultivates_the_Perspective-Taking_Disposition.

◆ Kaya, M. F. (2013). The effect of six thinking hats on student success in teaching subjects related to sustainable development in geography classes. *Theory and Practice, 13*(2). https://eric.ed.gov/?id=EJ1017274

SCAMPER

◆ Özyaprak, M. (2016). The effectiveness of SCAMPER technique on creative thinking skills. *Journal for the Education of Gifted Young Scientists, 4*, 31. https://doi.org/10.17478/JEGYS.2016116348.

◆ Wu, T., & Wu, Y., & Yu-Tzu Wu (2020). Applying project-based learning and SCAMPER teaching strategies in engineering education to explore the influence of creativity on cognition, personal motivation, and personality traits. *Thinking Skills and Creativity, 35*(1), 100631. https://doi.org/10.1016/j.tsc.2020.100631.

Synectics

◆ Kahn, A. A., & Mahmood, N. (2017). The role of the synectics model in enhancing students' understanding of geometrical concepts. *Journal of Research and Reflections, 2*(11), 253–264.

◆ Suratno, K. N., Yushardi, D., & Wicaksono, I. (2019). The effect of using synectics model on creative thinking and metacognition skills of junior high school students. *International Journal of Instruction, 12*(3). http://repository.unej.ac.id//handle/123456789/95172

Critical Thinking

◆ Abrami, P. C., Bernard, R. M., Borokhovski, E., Wade, A., Surkes, M. A., Tamim, R., & Zhang, D. (2008). Instructional interventions affecting critical thinking skills and dispositions: A stage 1 meta-analysis. *Review of Educational Research, 78*(4), 1102–1134. https://doi.org/10.3102/0034654308326084

◆ Little C. (2001). Reasoning as a key component of language arts curricula. *Journal of Secondary Gifted Education, 13*(2), 52–59. https://doi:10.4219/jsge-2002-366

◆ Reed, J. H. (1998). *Effect of a model for critical thinking on student achievement in primary source document analysis and interpretation, argumentative reasoning, critical thinking dispositions, and history content in a community college history course* (Order No. 9911510). [Doctoral Dissertation, University of South Florida]. https://www.proquest.com/docview/304454601?pq-origsite=gscholar&fromopenview=true

Metapatterns

◆ Bloom, J. W., & Volk, T. (2007). The use of metapatterns for research into complex systems of teaching, learning, and schooling. Part II: Applications. *Complicity: An International Journal of Complexity and Education, 4*(1), 45–68. http://ejournals.library.ualberta.ca/index.php/complicity/article/view/8760/7080.

Metacognitive Strategies

◆ Dhindsa, H. S., Makarimi-Kasimm, & Anderson, R. O. (2011). Constructivist-visual mind map teaching approach and the quality of students' cognitive structures. *Journal of Science Education and Technology, 20*, 186–200. https://doi.org/10.1007/s10956-010-9245-4

◆ Duckworth, A. L., Kirby, T., Gollwitzer, A., & Oettingen, G. (2013). From fantasy to action: Mental contrasting with implementation intentions (MCII) improves academic performance in children. *Social Psychological and Personality Science, 4*(6), 745–753. https://doi.org/10.1177/1948550613476307

◆ Harackiewicz, J. M., Canning, E. A., Tibbetts, Y., Priniski, S. J., & Hyde, J. S. (2016). Closing achievement gaps with a utility-value intervention: Disentangling race and social class. *Journal of Personality and Social Psychology, 111*(5), 745–765. https://doi.org/10.1037/pspp0000075.

Principles for Curriculum Design (Gifted)

◆ National Association for Gifted Children (2019). *2019 pre-K-grade 12 gifted programming standards.* www.nagc.org/resources-publications/ resources/national-standards-gifted-and-talented-education/pre-k-grade-12
◆ Stambaugh, T., & Mofield, E. (2022). *A teacher's guide to curriculum design for gifted and advanced learners: Advanced content models for differentiating curriculum.* Routledge Press.
◆ VanTassel-Baska, J. (2018). Achievement unlocked. Effective curriculum interventions with low-income students. *Gifted Child Quarterly, 62*(1), 68–82. https://doi.org/10.1177/0016986217738565

References

Adams, W., Wieman, C., & Schwartz, D. (2008). *Teaching expert thinking.* www. cwsei.ubc.ca/resources/files/Teaching_Expert_Thinking.pdf

Adler, M., & Gorman, W. (1990). *The great ideas: A syntopicon of great books of the western world* (Vols. I–III). Encyclopedia Britannica.

Anderson, E. F. (2015). Engaging and effective strategies for English language learners. In D. Sisk (Ed.), *Accelerating and extending literacy for diverse students* (pp. 66–83). Rowman & Littlefield.

Bateson, G. (1979). *Mind and nature: A necessary unity.* Bantam Books.

Beasley, J. G., Briggs, C., & Pennington, L. (2017). Bridging the gap 10 years later: A tool and technique to analyze and evaluate advanced academic curricular units. *Gifted Child Today, 40,* 48–58. https://doi. org/10.1177/1076217516675902

Black, B., Chislett, J., Thomson, A., Thwaites, G., & Thwaites, J. (2008). *Critical thinking—a definition and taxonomy for Cambridge assessment.* Research Matters. www.cambridgeassessment.org.uk/Images/480038-critical-thinking-a-definition-and-taxonomy-for-cambridge-assessment.pdf

Bransford, J. D., Brown, A. L., & Cocking, R. R. (2000). *How people learn: Brain, mind, experience, and school.* National Academy Press.

Briggs, C. J., Reis, S. M., & Sullivan, E. E. (2008). A national view of promising programs and practices for culturally, linguistically, and ethnically diverse gifted and talented students. *Gifted Child Quarterly, 52*(2), 131–145. https://doi.org/ 10.1177/0016986208316037

Buck, J. N. (1970). *The House-Tree-Person technique. Revised manual.* Western Psychological Services.

Buzan, T., & Buzan, B. (1993). *The mind map book: How to use radiant thinking to maximize your brain's untapped potential.* Plume.

Cameron, L. (2013). Metaphors in the learning of science: A discourse focus. *British Educational Research Journal,* 673–688. https://doi.org/ 10.1080/0141192022000015534

Chi, M. T. H., Glaser, R., & Fall, M. J. (1988). *The nature of expertise.* Lawrence Erlbaum Associates.

Cohen, G. L., Steele, C. M., & Ross, L. D. (1999). The mentor's dilemma: Providing critical feedback across the racial divide. *Personality and Social Psychology Bulletin, 25*(10), 1302–1318.

College of William and Mary/Center for Gifted Education (2008). *What's the matter? A physical science unit for high-ability learners in Grades 2–3* (William & Mary Units). Prufrock Press/Routledge.

de Bono, E. (1992). *Serious creativity.* Harper Collins.

de Bono, E. (1994). *de Bono's thinking course.* International Center for Creative Thinking.

de Bono, E. (2016). *Six thinking hats.* Penguin. (Original work published 1985)

Doubet, K. J., & Hockett, J. A. (2015). *Differentiation in middle and high school: Strategies to engage all learners.* ASCD.

Durik, A. M., Shechter, O. G., Noh, M., Rozek, C. S., & Harackiewicz, J. M. (2015). What if I can't? Success expectancies moderate the effects of utility value information on situational interest and performance. *Motivation and Emotion, 39*(1), 104–118. https://doi.org/10.1007/s11031-014-9419-0

Eberle, B. (2008). *Scamper: Creative games and activities for imagination development.* Prufrock Press.

Erickson, H. L. (2007). *Concept-based curriculum and instruction for the thinking classroom.* Corwin Press.

Fisher, D., Frey, N., Quaglia, R. J., Smith, D., & Lande, L. L. (2018). *Engagement by design: Creating learning environments where students thrive.* Corwin.

Ford, D. Y. (2011). *Multicultural gifted education* (2nd ed.). Prufrock Press.

Gay, G. (2018). *Culturally responsive teaching: Theory, research, and practice.* Teacher's College Press.

Gordon, W. (1961). *Synectics.* Harper and Row.

Guilford, J. P. (1967). *The nature of human intelligence.* McGraw-Hill.

Harackiewicz, J. M., Canning, E. A., Tibbetts, Y., Priniski, S. J., & Hyde, J. S. (2016). Closing achievement gaps with a utility-value intervention: Disentangling race and social class. *Journal of Personality and Social Psychology, 111*(5), 745–765. https://doi.org/10.1037/pspp0000075.

Hattie, J. (2012). *Visible learning for teachers: Maximizing impact on learning.* Routledge.

Hattie, J. (2017). *Visible learning MetaX.* https://www.visiblelearningmetax.com/Influences

Hattie, J., Fisher, D., & Frey, N. (2017). *Visible learning for mathematics: What works best to optimize student learning.* Corwin.

Hess, K., Jones, B. S., Carlock, D., & Walkup, J. R. (2009). *Cognitive rigor: Blending the strengths of Bloom's taxonomy and Webb's depth of knowledge to enhance classroom-level processes.* www.standardsco.com/PDF /Cognitive_Rigor_Paper.pdf

Hockett, J. A., & Brighton, C. M. (2016). General curriculum design: Principles and best practices. In K. R. Stephens & F. A. Karnes (Eds.), *Introduction to curriculum design in gifted education* (pp. 41–62). Prufrock Press.

Hsu, Y. (2006). The effects of metaphors on novice and expert learners' performance and mental model development. *Interacting with Computers, 18*, 770–792. https://doi.org/10.1016/j.intcom.2005.10.008

Kaplan, S. (2009). Layering differentiated curricula for the gifted and talented. In F. A. Karnes & S. M. Bean (Eds.), *Methods and materials for teaching the gifted* (3rd ed., pp. 107–156). Prufrock Press.

Kettler, T. (2016). Curriculum design in an era of ubiquitous information and technology. In T. Kettler (Ed.), *Modern curriculum for gifted and advanced academic students* (pp. 3–21). Prufrock Press.

Kettler, T., Lamb, K. N., & Mullet, D. R. (2018). *Developing creativity in the classroom: Learning and innovation for 21st-century schools.* Prufrock Press.

Lekshmi, D. (2020). Schema mental models and learning: An overview. *Journal of Critical Reviews, 7*(15), 2800–2807. https://doi.10.31838/jcr.07.15.382

Little, C. (2001). Reasoning as a key component of language arts curricula. *Journal of Secondary Gifted Education, 13*(2), 52–59. https://doi:10.4219/jsge-2002-366

Luft, J., & Ingram, H. (1955). *The Johari Window: A graphic model for interpersonal relations.* University of California-Los Angeles Western Training Lab.

Maker, C. J. (1982). *Curriculum development for the gifted.* Aspen.

Matthews, M. S., & Castellano, J. A. (2014). *Developing English language learners' talents: Identifying and nurturing potential* [Webinar]. National Association for Gifted Children. www.nagc.org/demand-learning

McTighe, J., & Silver, H. F. (2020). *Teaching for deeper learning: Tools to engage students in meaning making.* ASCD.

McTighe, J., & Wiggins, G. (2012). *The understanding by design guide to creating high-quality units.* ASCD.

McTighe, J., & Wiggins, G. (2013). *Essential questions: Opening doors to student understanding.* ASCD.

Mindtools (n.d.). *5 Whys: Getting to the root of a problem quickly.* www.mindtools.com/pages/article/newTMC_5W.htm

Mofield, E. (2020). Teaching psychosocial skills and habits of achievement. In P. Olszewski-Kubilius & T. Stambaugh (Eds.), *Unlocking potential: Identifying and serving students from low-income households* (pp. 241–262). Prufrock Press.

Mofield, E., & Parker Peters, M. (2018). *Teaching tenacity, resilience, and a drive for excellence: Lessons for social-emotional learning.* Prufrock Press.

Mofield, E., & Phelps, V. (2020). *Collaboration, coteaching, and coaching in gifted education: Sharing strategies to support gifted learners.* Prufrock Press.

National Association for Gifted Children (2019). *2019 pre-K-grade 12 gifted programming standards.* www.nagc.org/resources-publications/resources/national-standards-gifted-and-talented-education/pre-k-grade-12

Oettingen, G., & Gollwitzer, P. M. (2010). Strategies of setting and implementing goals: Mental contrasting and implementation intentions. In J. E. Maddux & J. P. Tangney (Eds.), *Social psychological foundations of clinical psychology* (pp. 114–135). Guilford Press.

Passow, A. H. (1982). Differentiated curricula for the gifted/talented: A point of view. In S. Kaplan, A. H. Passow, P. H. Phenix, S. M. Reis, J. S. Renzulli, I. Sato, ... V. S. Ward (Eds.), *Curricula for the gifted* (pp. 4–20). National/State Leadership Institute on the Gifted/Talented.

Paul, R., & Elder, L. (2019). *Critical thinking: Tools for taking charge of your learning and your life* (3rd ed.). Pearson.

Persky, A. M., & Robinson, J. D. (2017). Moving from novice to expertise and its implications for instruction. *American Journal of Pharmaceutical Education, 81,* 6065. https://doi.org/10.5688/ajpe6065

Phenix, P. H. (1964). *Realms of meaning.* McGraw-Hill.

Potash, B. (2020, September 11). *Hexagonal thinking: A colorful tool for discussion. Cult of pedagogy.* www.cultofpedagogy.com/hexagonal-thinking/

Project Zero (2019). *The tug of war thinking routine.* Research center at the Harvard Graduate School of Education. www.pz.harvard.edu/resources/tug-of-war

Purdue Online Writing Lab (n.d.a). *Classical argument.* Purdue OWL. https://owl.purdue.edu/owl/general_writing/academic_writing/historical_perspectives_on_argumentation/classical_argument.html

Purdue Online Writing Lab (n.d.b). *Rogerian argument.* Purdue OWL. https://owl.purdue.edu/owl/general_writing/academic_writing/historical_perspectives_on_argumentation/rogerian_argument.html.

Ritchhart, R., Church, M., & Morrison, K. (2011). *Making thinking visible: How to promote engagement, understanding, and independence for all learners.* Jossey Bass.

Roukes, N. (1988). *Design synectics: Stimulating creativity in design.* Davis Publications.

Sather, T. (1999). *Pros and cons: A debater's handbook.* Taylor & Francis.

Schwartz, H. (2019). *Connected teaching: Relationship, power, and mattering in higher education.* Stylus Publishing.

Senge, P. (1990). *The fifth discipline: The art and practice of the learning organization* (revised and updated ed.). Random House.

Silver, H. F., & Perini, M. J. (2010). *Classroom curriculum design: How strategic units improve instruction and engage students in meaningful learning.* Thoughtful Education Press.

Simpson, H. K., & Pellegrino, J. W. (1993). Descriptive models in learning command languages. *Journal of Educational Psychology, 85,* 539–550. https://doi.org/10.1037/0022-0663.85.3.539

Stambaugh, T. (2018). Curriculum and instruction within a talent develop-ment framework. In P. Olszewski-Kubilius, R. F. Subotnik, & F. C. Worrell (Eds.), *Talent development as a framework for gifted education: Implications for best practices and applications in school* (pp. 95–127). Prufrock Press.

Stambaugh, T., & Mofield, E. (2018). *Space, structure, and story: Integrated sci-ence and ELA lessons for gifted and advanced learners in grades 4–6*. Prufrock Press.

Stambaugh, T., & Mofield, E. (2022). *A teacher's guide to curriculum design for gifted and advanced learners: Advanced content models for differentiating cur-riculum*. Routledge Press.

Statistica (n.d.). *Weekly time spent playing video games in the United States as of January 2021*. https://www.statista.com/statistics/936654/weekly-time-spent-playing-video-games-usa/

Stern, J., Ferraro, K., Duncan, K., & Aleo, T. (2021). *Learning that transfers: Designing curriculum for a changing world*. Corwin Press.

Sternberg, R. J. (1997). A triarchic view of giftedness: Theory and practice. In N. Coleangelo & G. Davis (Eds.), *Handbook of gifted education* (pp. 43–53). Allyn & Bacon.

Subotnik, R. F., Olszewski-Kubilius, P., & Worrell, F. C. (2011). Rethinking giftedness and gifted education: A proposed direction forward based on psychological science. *Psychological Science in the Public Interest, 12,* 3–54.

SWOT Analysis Not Simple (2020, October 5). *In wikipedia commons.* https://commons.wikimedia.org/wiki/File:SWOT_Analysis_ssw_1.png

Taba, H., Durkin, M. C., Fraenkel, J. R., & McNaughton, A. H. (1971). *A teach-er's handbook to elementary social studies: An inductive approach* (2nd ed.). Addison-Wesley.

Tomlinson, C. A. (2004). *How to differentiate instruction in mixed ability class-rooms*. ASCD.

Tomlinson, C. A., Kaplan, S., Renzulli, J., Purcell, J., Leppein, J., & Burns, D. (2002). *The parallel curriculum: A design to develop high potential and challenge high-ability learners*. Corwin Press (NAGC Publication).

Torrance, E. P. (1962). *Guiding creative talent*. Prentice Hall.

VanTassel-Baska, J. (2018). Achievement unlocked. Effective curriculum inter-ventions with low-income students. *Gifted Child Quarterly, 62*(1), 68–82. https://doi.org/10.1177/0016986217738565

VanTassel-Baska, J., & Baska, A. (2019). *Curriculum planning and instructional design for gifted learners* (3rd ed.). Prufrock Press.

VanTassel-Baska, J., Hubbard, G. F., & Robbins, J. I. (2020). Differentiation of instruction for gifted learners: Collated evaluative studies of teacher classroom practices. *Roeper Review, 42*(3), 153–164. https://doi.org/10.1080/02783193.2020.1765919

VanTassel-Baska, J., & Stambaugh, T. (2006). *Comprehensive curriculum for gifted learners* (3rd ed.). Pearson.

Volk, T. (1995). *Metapatterns: Across space, time, and mind.* Columbia University Press.

Volk, T., & Bloom, J. W. (2007). The use of metapatterns for research into complex systems of teaching, learning, and schooling. *Complicity: An International Journal of Complexity and Education, 4*(1), 25–43. https://doi.org/10.29173/cmplct8759

Webb, N. (1997). *Research monograph number 6: "Criteria for alignment of expectations and assessments on mathematics and science education.* CCSSO.

Weinstein, Y., Madan, C., & Sumeracki, M. (2018). Teaching the science of learning. *Cognitive Research: Principles and Implications. 3*(2), 1–17. https://doi.org/10.1186/s41235-017-0087-y

WIDA Consortium (2014). *The 2012 amplification of the English language development standards: Kindergarten—grade 12.* WIDA. https://wida.wisc.edu/sites/default/files/resource/2012-ELD-Standards.pdf

Wiederhold, C., & Kagan, S. (1998). *Cooperative learning and higher-level thinking: The Q-Matrix.* Kagan Publishing.

Wigfield, A., & Eccles, J. S. (1992). The development of achievement task values: A theoretical analysis. *Developmental Review, 12*(3), 265–310. https://doi.org/10.1016/0273-2297(92)90011-P

Wigfield, A., & Eccles, J. S. (2000). Expectancy—value theory of achievement motivation. *Contemporary Educational Psychology, 25*(1), 68–81. https://doi.org/10.1006/ceps.1999.1015

Winebrenner, S. (2001). *Teaching gifted kids in the regular classroom.* Free Spirit Press.

World Economic Forum (2020). *Future of jobs report.* www.weforum.org/reports/the-future-of-jobs-report-2020

Made in the USA
Coppell, TX
10 April 2024

31106893R10109